ABOUT THE AUTHOR

John Bell has worked for over 30 years in diplomacy and mediation in the Middle East, including with the United Nations, the Canadian government and international NGOs. He is today the Director of The Conciliators Guild, an organization that aims to liberate political fixations by spreading knowledge about the critical underlying motivations behind much of our behaviour. He is also co-founder of the Jerusalem Old City Initiative, an effort to find creative options for this contentious issue, and has been published widely on Middle East politics in newspapers, journals and websites around the world. He currently resides near Oxford in the United Kingdom.

HOW TO TAME THE POLITICAL ANIMAL

HOW TO TAME THE POLITICAL ANIMAL

THE MISSING PIECE

JOHN BELL

Human Givens
Publishing

Human Givens
Publishing

First published in Great Britain in 2021

Published by HG Publishing, an imprint of Human Givens Publishing Ltd.,
Chalvington, East Sussex, BN27 3TD, United Kingdom.
www.humangivens.com/publications

A catalogue record for this book is available from the British Library.

ISBN (p): 978-1-899398-99-7
ISBN (e): 978-1-899398-98-0

Cover design by Benjamin Brown
Index by Caroline Diepeveen
Printed and bound in Great Britain.

CONTENTS

Preface
THE GOLDEN GATE

And the first age was Gold,
Without laws, without laws' enforcers
This age understood and obeyed
What had created it,
Listening deeply, man kept faith with the source.

– Ovid, *Metamorphoses* [1]

IN THE famed Eastern wall of the Old City of Jerusalem, below the Temple Mount/Haram Al-Sharif, stands the Golden Gate. Unlike the other seven gates of Jerusalem, it has been sealed shut for centuries. This is where some Jews and Muslims believe the Messiah, or the Mahdi, will enter the city at the end of time.

The idea of the coming Messiah lives in the minds of millions of Jews, Muslims, and Christians around the world. Each of these faiths is wedded to a pattern of belief about the path to the One God, the story of a glorious past, or a more glorious Messianic future. Indeed, Jews and Arabs fight over the land called Palestine, Israel, the Holy Land, while others, Shia, Sunni and Kurd, struggle with each other for control and survival – and the Golden Gate remains firmly shut.

The grab for Jerusalem, for the exclusive right to the Golden

Gate, is a great symbol of our age. The Middle East itself represents the arena where our most intense attachments to the holy smoke, religion and tribes, and their heady intermingling are playing out. This crucible is in all of us, we are all members of nations, ways of life and prejudices – tribes – to which we are dearly attached, and which permit us to see some as kin, but most as strangers.

And it is this stranger that confuses, that we wish off our land and that, at the best of times, is tolerated. It is 'the one who does not belong' that is the centre of many of our political controversies.

In no region does man suffer more from these afflictions than the Middle East. It is there that, since the capture of Jericho by the Hebrews, the Christian Crusades of the 12th century, the Islamic Conquest, to today's wars between Arabs and Israelis, Shia and Sunni, and the rise of radicalism, we see people fight for power and control, over apparently sacred land and scriptures, for what belongs to them, and only them.

This endless battle with the outsider – over resources, land and identity – is a large part of history. As English philosopher Thomas Hobbes put it, life outside of society could be "solitary, poor, nasty, brutish and short", and thus we must make adaptations, including sometimes by clinging tightly to our groups. Too often, when confronted by the stranger, especially one that threatens us, the answer is 'realpolitik' (the Fight!), and many glory in that scenario. However, our take on the stranger may be inaccurate, even illusory, and we may create an enemy of a stranger by the way we deal with him or her.

The outstanding irony is that it is from the Middle East that a new more accepting view of the stranger often came. These messages are called scriptures: Torah, Gospel and Koran. Despite their complexities and mixtures of meanings, these books do often speak of the development of openness, trust, and even forgiveness of the stranger in our midst. They certainly speak of a broader outlook on life that can lead to greater wisdom in our actions.

The process of lessening strife with an outsider may be in looking to ourselves for the answers – and not to the stranger. A greater understanding of the fundamental unit of society that is behind the chaos and conflict: the human being, will be the entry ticket for achieving a humanity that is more 'whole,' and a less fragmented – and more coherent – Middle East, or elsewhere for that matter. A better grasp of human nature can be the source of stability, contentment and great meaning and achievement in our lives – if we bother to understand and master it.

This book is about this missing piece, that most human of dimensions that is at the centre of all our politics, and yet often casually ignored. It is about what lies *behind* our actions, basic and powerful drives that sideline common sense, and are ignored at our peril. They impel great flights of fancy through our tribal, national and ideological groups. They thrive in a world of 'us and them,' misguided trajectories of cultural identity. In extremis, these motives evolve into radicalized and violent behaviour of unfathomable strains. One term for it is simply our 'ego,' but it is more than that, it is what drives us to survive and thrive.

So, why has this not been discovered before? The irony is that it has been with us all along, all around us and in us. We can readily believe the ego is active in others, but the last place we will want to look for answers is in ourselves.

It is not a coincidence that it has been said that "the summary of the advice of all prophets is this: find yourself a mirror."[2] The great faiths and philosophies have always said the answer was in us. The maxim "know thyself" was inscribed in the forecourt of the Temple of Apollo at Delphi (known as the

Delphic Oracle). The full expression, derived from Ancient Egypt, is "know thyself, and you are going to know the gods."

It is from the Middle East that, once upon a time, man has often articulated his desire to gain greater understanding and live a rich and freer existence amidst the nastiness and brevity of it all. It may be the ironic greed for an exclusive hold on these 'truths' that brings us to where we are: in chaos and under the constant threat of devastating war and conflict.

The desire for a truthful life marks the Middle East just as much as violence and intolerance and, despite its tragic present, may point to its ultimate destination. Not a future of apocalypse or paradise, but something less dreamy.

The Golden Gate has another name; it is also called Bab Ar-Rahmeh, Sha'ar HaRachamim, or the Gate of Mercy. That gate may indeed remain shut until the hearts and minds of men and women, Jews, Arabs or others open a bit wider with greater knowledge to the stranger in their midst – and maybe that is all there is to the arrival of a messiah.

Who or what can give me the power of transforming a mirror into a doorway?

– Dag Hammarskjold, *Markings* [1]

PART I

———

ADVENTURES ON A BLUE LINE

The preservation of self-image is more important than self-preservation.

– Arthur Deikman, *Them and Us: Cult Thinking
and the Terrorist Threat* [1]

THE DEMON AND
THE HAPPY COUPLE

"There was once a happily married couple whom a demon decided to separate. He went first to the wife, in the guise of an old woman, and muttered that her spouse was behaving in a distraught fashion because he was in love with another woman. Then he went to the husband, in the form of a palmist, and told him that his wife was secretly involved with another man.

"When the husband went home from his work that evening, it was quite natural that he should be uncomfortable with his wife, and she with him. Because of this tension, however, each concluded that there must be some truth in what he or she had been told.

"Of course, they were not certain about their suspicions; and the demon knew this and developed another phase of his attack. He told the woman that he had a spell that would reclaim her husband's fidelity. 'This,' he said, 'can be accomplished by cutting three hairs from his beard. Here is a razor with which to do it.'

"Now he told the husband, who was starting to question the truth of the soothsayer's readings, that his wife would attempt to kill him that very night.

"When the man got home, his wife asked him to lie down and rest and he did so, pretending to go to sleep. As soon as she thought it was safe, she took out the razor and advanced upon him with it – and the husband opened his eyes to see this 'proof' of her murderous intentions.

"The husband, so continues the story, killed his wife, and the neighbours, alarmed and infuriated and panicking, killed him.

"Finally, everyone in their town took sides and there was a clash in which almost everyone there was also killed." [1]

ORIGINS:
THE DOG RIVER TABLETS

To mourn a mischief that is past and gone is the next way to draw new mischief on.

– Shakespeare, *Othello* (Act I, Scene iii) [1]

I WOULD arrive to the Middle East on a jet plane, and the descent would begin a few hundred kilometres out. Whether I was heading for Tel Aviv, Beirut, or Cairo, I would tell myself, "I am now entering the *asfourieh*, 'the place of the birds' in Arabic, but also the name of a mental hospital in Beirut that became the term for all such institutions.

Ironically, I sought this madness, madly. Ever since a Scandinavian Airlines DC-9 had taken my family from Beirut to start a new life in Canada in 1968, I had plotted my return. Whether in daydreams or reading about its ancient or modern history, or family connections, I maintained a lingering link.

I was away from the region from 1974 until 1993, primarily due to the Lebanese civil war. In 1986, at the exuberant age of 26, I had threatened to go to Lebanon, but my parents went crazy with fear. So, I went to El Salvador instead to visit friends working with the United Nations High Commissioner for Refugees (UNHCR), where I heard the thud of artillery, and saw battle-weary soldiers returning from the front, the dead gaze of war in their eyes. El Salvador in the 1980s was as dangerous as Lebanon – although not in the minds of my parents. But, in the end, return to the Middle East I did, over and over again, as a diplomat and tourist, visiting family, and always seeking... something. I did not originally know quite what. A romantic return 'home' to my origins? Certainly, I was on a trip, personal, political, and social.

When my family left Lebanon for good in 1968, and that aircraft took off from Beirut to Istanbul, and from there to Vienna, London, Copenhagen and my future home, Canada, I was filled with childhood memories. Redolent with melancholia, I left a land that I loved. The smell of jasmine on the stairway leading to my grandparents' house, the fresh air of a land named after its mountains' snow,[2] the chaos of the souks – these were all 'souvenirs' that I took with me to Canada, alongside a sense of lost home that ended up compelling me to return.

Before that departure, we lived in Tripoli, Lebanon, where we had a comfortable life. We would also often travel the coastal road to Sidon, my mother's hometown, to spend the weekend at my grandparents' hilltop home overlooking the sea.

My grandfather, Azar Nahas, was a classic patriarch who mixed the masculine ethos of his world with a strong instinct for what was good and necessary. He was a respected *mukhtar* (community leader) in Sidon. I still link him with the smell of charcoal burning the Persian tobacco of his *argileh* (or water pipe) that bubbled in the morning and, again, in the evening. We would go on that drive to Sidon every couple of weeks and we looked forward to it with delight. It was a chance to meet cousins and have some great food.

On the way, we passed through a series of rock outcroppings that reached into the sea. These massifs, from Ras Chekka after Tripoli to Ras Naqoura on the border with Israel, create coves and bays that naturally separate areas or districts of Lebanon. They also serve to channel locals out to the sea rather than towards the next valley, a geography that affects the Lebanese, defining the local 'geopolitics' – how the people interact, and how segmented they became.

There were tunnels carved into these rocks, and I enjoyed the trip into their short, dark passage. A famous one, north of Beirut, is known as the Dog River tunnel (or Nahr El Kalb) after the waters that flow by it into the Mediterranean. What was remarkable was that, carved into its northern side were plaques from history.

The Dog River was a key passage for any army moving along the Lebanese coast. It was narrow, difficult to cross and inspired the conquerors to chisel their passage in stone once they succeeded. Each conqueror left a mark announcing his arrival and, of course, imitating his predecessor: Ramses II, Nebuchadnezzar, Alexander the Great, the Roman emperor Caracalla, Salah al-Din and Napoleon III of France – they were all here. I imagined being a soldier in their armies, especially the ancient Egyptians in their rickety, elegant chariots, working to get around the rock. One wrong move, and it was into the sea.

When I was older, I realized that the tablets at the Dog River spoke to the multi-layered history of the region: "The Middle East is *the* invaded civilization: it is the occupied territory par excellence." [3]

The region stands at the intersection of three continents. It has served as a cultural and commercial crossroads between Asia, Europe, and Africa, a permanent distribution network of scriptures, goods, gods and people. It was somewhat unavoidable that it would become *the* invaded land; its location demanded it. But, as a result, all cultures here have a memory of conquest and violence.

Cities like Sidon, Jericho, and Aleppo contain the sediments of destruction beneath today's streets. There, layers of soot mark burning and looting, and the violent deaths of loved ones. The Mongol invasions, the rule of the Byzantines, the cruelty of the Crusaders, the arrival of the Islamic faith, each left its impact on the local culture – and on traumatized inhabitants.

Only later was I to learn that the anxiety and high emotion that characterizes the people of the region, and that I shared, were partly the result of defence reflexes provoked by millennia of threat. The Middle East knows vulnerability well, the responses are woven into people's daily affairs, and their culture.

In such a situation, tight identification with one's group became crucial. Who could you rely upon to survive except kin and blood relatives? The state was distant, corrupt and often oppressive. If you and your local group did not stick together, the game was over. The significance of all this was to make sense to me years later.

However, as a result, past patterns and old mechanisms of survival were repeated, but they had a price: "to mourn a mischief that is past and gone is the next way to draw new mischief on." And mischief there was to be.

"A STORM OF EMOTIONS…
A TEMPEST OF CAPRICES"

I WAS always a bit of a radical. I wanted to quit university and play in a punk band, an idea that thankfully failed miserably. But, I always wanted to get to the root of things, a factor that has influenced the writing of this book. Given I come from the Middle East, before going any further, it might be good to lay out my own roots, and the origins of my family, because that was to influence who I was to become, and how I became interested in a diplomatic career in the Middle East.

In a way, it all started with Robert Smith Bell, my American grandfather, and his story begins not in the east, but in Philadelphia, USA. During the First World War, R.S. Bell, moved from there to Montreal, Canada, probably because he had lost his American family in an epidemic. There, he joined the British army to fight in World War I. He was first sent to Europe, where he was wounded, before ending up with General Allenby in Palestine.[1] He arrived just as the Balfour Declaration of 1917–18 was made.[2]

There, in Palestine, he fell in love with and married a local woman, Emily Cohen, who happened to be a Jew from the Galilean village of Shef'amer. Her father was a rabbi there and she was a local who spoke Arabic and, in a sense, was as Palestinian as Yasser Arafat – if a little prettier. Her mother's side, the

Hassans, were traders in cloth in Haifa. Emily and Robert raised a family in Haifa, including my father, Jack. My dad was born in Amman in 1921 because at the time his father was working there, responsible for repairing the railway that his colleague, Lawrence of Arabia, had blown up only a few years before.

Emily grew up in an Arab culture before the power of Zionism came from Europe to the Middle East, and not only were the Palestinians in trouble, but so was my grandmother. In 1948, the year Israel was created, the Zionists kicked her and my father's family out of their home on the slopes of Mount Carmel (my grandfather had passed away). The Zionists saw them as being too close to Arabs, not Zionist enough.

Also in 1948, my father left Haifa for Lebanon. He was employed by the Iraqi Petroleum Company, which moved its offices and oil refinery from Palestine to Lebanon because the Iraqis had shut off the tap to Haifa, to what was to imminently become Israel. When my father entered Lebanon, the authorities registered him as a Palestinian because the only ID that he carried was a British Mandate Palestine passport. Mr. Bell, the Palestinian. Since he only held a British Mandate Palestine passport, my birth certificate, from the American University Hospital in Beirut, states that my nationality is Palestinian. As there is officially no Palestine, everyone in my family except my mother was stateless.

My mother, Lily Nahas, is Lebanese through and through. She is from Saida and its surroundings, some of her ancestry hailing from the mostly Shia village of Jbe' that traditionally had two Christian families, the Haddads and the Nahas. Although there are also reports of Greek somewhere on her side, we'll keep it simple. She also left her home in Saida to be educated in Beirut and then to move and work in the US, a bold step for a woman in that era and of that cultural background.

Technically, as a Palestinian living in Lebanon, and one

quarter Jewish, I can go to Israel/Palestine on both the Palestinian right of return and the Israeli right of return. However, I am content with my Canadian passport.

Through this complex history, my family and my future were inextricably tied to the developments of Middle East history, its ebbs and flows shaped our lives and marked our destiny.

- 1917, Balfour Declaration, my grandfather arrives in Middle East;

- 1948, my father leaves Palestine for Lebanon;

- 1967, the Six Day War and creeping regional trouble ended up defining our future.

My memories of that war are of my parents putting up blue-tinted glass on our windows at night in Tripoli, Lebanon, so that Israeli military jets could not see the city's lights. In that defeat, angry Nasserists also found threat in anything with an imperial tinge, including an Anglo-Imperial family name of Bell. So, our family had to escape to my grandfather's home in Saida. That was when the straw landed on the camel's back, and my parents took the decision to emigrate.[3]

In November 1968, we (Jack and Lily, and their children, Robert, Joyce, John and Michael) left Lebanon for good, and adapted to a new world. Canada did become home, indeed, a place to develop and thrive. However, the Six Day War was not only a turning point for my family, it was an axis upon which the region turned.

1967 was a door onto a 'new Middle East.' Some actors exited, while others entered with vehemence. For the Arabs, it meant that nationalist dreams were destroyed in a few days. The Arab world would never be the same after that debacle; an idealistic bubble had burst, leaving an aching hole that was to be filled by the fantasies of extremists or the cheap corruption of the less fanciful. For Israelis, it was quite the reverse, a dream had been fulfilled against all odds.

Before the war, on the eve of Israeli Independence Day in May 1967, Rabbi Tzvi Yehuda Kook gave a sermon to a group of his rabbinical students. "He described his profound disappointment in the 1947 UN partition plan, and the fact that the Jews had not been awarded Biblical places like Hebron, where the Patriarchs are buried, and Shiloh, the centre of Jewish worship before the building of the First Temple. 'I succumbed to this feeling of shock, my body torn to shreds, I had nothing to celebrate,' he said."[4] Three weeks later, Israel captured Sinai, the West Bank, Gaza, the Golan Heights, East Jerusalem – as well as all the holy sites that Rabbi Kook had longed for.

When the Israeli army took the walled Old City of Jerusalem from the Jordanians, a platoon commander sent a jeep to bring Kook to the Western Wall. There, the rabbi exclaimed, "We hereby inform the people of Israel and the entire world that under heavenly command we have just returned home in the elevations of holiness and our holy city. We shall never move out of here."[5]

The conquest of the West Bank and Jerusalem was like a 'godsend'. A small nation had gained victory over several larger ones; David had slain Goliath and, for some, this miracle could only be divinely ordained, a confirmation of their covenant with a deity that preferred their people and mission over others. Indeed, the 1967 war left Israel with much land to expand into, or trade off in negotiations – and the Arab world in tatters. It was the Egyptian air force, not Rabbi Kook, that had been shredded. The political motivations behind the 1967 war were however more irrational than we think – and this is where our tale really begins.

Israeli journalist Uzi Benziman has researched the Israeli government decision to conquer East Jerusalem in 1967. He concluded that the decision was not, as is often presumed, based on an existential threat to Israel or a need for greater security. Instead, it seems it was taken "primarily for emotional reasons."[6] Like the good rabbi, some Israeli leaders felt that the decision during the 1948 war to avoid taking the Old City of Jerusalem and all that it contained – the core of Jewish heritage – had to be reversed.

As a result, after the conquest, "Jerusalem was unified in the wake of a storm of emotions, not to say a tempest of caprices, that took hold of a small number of decision makers in the government and the Israeli Defence Forces (IDF), and drove them to transform radically the situation in the Middle East."[7]

A storm of emotions, a tempest of caprices. Emotional fixations are very human, yet they were also the central issue in the region. We could try to skirt around or deny them, but if we did not attend to them properly, we would be left floundering, unable to find a positive path forward.

These fixations can be seen as a form of self-centredness, a mind that ignores all else around it to seek its own ends (and thereby creates conflict). But let's use a short form right off the bat: the ego, the sense that "I", and my needs, are more important than anything or anyone else.

JIBRIL AND PUFF THE MAGIC DRAGON

LIFE IN CANADA was good. My father once told me that it was 'as good as it gets' and indeed it is a country with far fewer identity fixations than the Middle East. However, I thought we could get better, and thus my insistence on returning to the region to jump right back into those identity fixations.

The late 1980s found me working in finance at the Canadian Tire Corporation in pleasant Toronto. I was a semi-happy yuppie with a Baltic Blue BMW, enjoying the finer restaurants of the city, when I learned that I had been accepted into the Canadian Foreign Service. I had toyed with other career paths, and considered pursuing a PhD in philosophy, but my passion for the region won out. I was insistent about the return 'home.'

After a few minutes of reflection on whether to take the job and a major pay cut, I told my Canadian Tire colleagues, on a hunch, that I was going to end up in Cairo. I had achieved my mission, and it was to be the Middle East for a couple of decades ahead. I began my career as a Canadian diplomat in 1991, and, as luck would have it, after a stint in Ottawa, I did indeed end up serving in Cairo.

Before Egypt, in September 1993, I arrived for the first time in Israel/Palestine/the Holy Land on my first diplomatic mission. A Canadian Embassy driver picked me up from Ben

Gurion airport and drove me to Jerusalem. Discovering that I spoke Arabic, the fellow started telling me in obscene and graphic detail about his sexual exploits, continuing the pornographic deluge all the way up the hills to Jerusalem. I tried hard to shut out the images he was projecting, and focused on the mountain air and the unique smell of pine and rosemary that mark the entrance to the holy city.

The very next day, September 3, 1993, I woke up at the American Colony Hotel to the news of the signing in Washington D.C. of the Oslo Accords, a set of agreements (named after Norway's capital, where the secret negotiations had been carried out) between Israel and the PLO (Palestinian Liberation Organization). It was a huge event. Suddenly, the unthinkable seemed possible. It led to giddy times laced with sincere hope, as barriers between enemies fell. Many felt that peace was at hand; early on in my career, things were looking up.

I shared in the atmosphere, but I also had doubts that a deal forged in Oslo would hold up in the rough and tumble of the Middle East. I shared my doubts with colleagues at the Canadian Foreign Ministry but, in their excitement, they didn't take my concerns too seriously.

I worked for many years on the issue of Israel-Palestine and, while doing that, the American Colony Hotel in Jerusalem became my home away from home. It is an old Palestinian mansion that was converted into an office for American missionaries in the 19th century, and later transformed into a wonderful hotel with a courtyard full of olive trees, flowers, and tiled tables.

Although it has lost much of its mystique, the American Colony still serves as the meeting point for Israelis and Palestinians, journalists, and diplomats for discussions on their neverending story. I was one of the diplomats that gathered there and, one day, I was sitting in the lobby of that hotel with Jibril Rajoub, a former West Bank strongman, also known as Abu

Rami. He had become sports czar for the Palestinian Authority and head of the Palestinian Football Association and Olympic Committee – positions that permitted him to channel his national ardour into constructive pursuits, and to attend sports matches as a local warlord – or god.

One time I had attended a football match with Jibril on the outskirts of Jerusalem. The stadium was lined on two sides by the wall that the Israelis had built to keep the Palestinians out. If you kicked the ball hard enough for it to go over the wall, fetching it back would be a problem.

On that occasion I was watching a local match with Abu Rami in the VIP space at the centre of the stadium, a balcony like Caesar's at the Coliseum but without velvet curtains and royal décor, when a fight broke out on the pitch. Suddenly, the President of the Palestinian Football Association leapt out of his seat and descended onto the field. Abu Rami himself separated the fighting players and got the match back on track. It is unlikely that the head of the Fédération Internationale de Football Association (FIFA) would have done that anytime soon; Jibril Rajoub has a lot of street cred.

Indeed, Abu Rami scares the hell out of people. He's a big man with a loud, gravelly voice reminiscent of a character from the American crime drama series *The Sopranos*. I have seen his growl make ambassadors and generals quake.[1]

As I was sitting with him at the American Colony Hotel, I saw three Americans across the lobby: an elderly balding man with long white hair, a younger woman in a summer dress, and a middle-aged man with crisp, preppie looks. As the three were talking, the elderly man pulled out a guitar, and began to strum and sing. The song was "Puff the Magic Dragon," a great melody that thrusts one into childish daze, purple rabbits, magic toadstools and all.

Jibril was oblivious of the event; I am sure he had never

heard of the song.[2] I, however, listened to the singer across the lobby with both surprise and pleasure. When one of the other two called him Peter, I realized he was none other than Peter from Peter, Paul and Mary, the group that had originally composed and performed the tune in the 1960s. Lo and behold, it turned out that Peter and friends were in Jerusalem on a peace mission.

The moment crystallized.

Here I was with Jibril Rajoub, tough guy who had spent years in jail, and for whom hard security - jail, police and intelligence services - was a familiar and essential aspect of the Middle East. Across the lobby were the Puff the Magic Dragon singers, for whom peace was about soft feelings, woolly goodwill and wishful thinking, which was also the premise of many peace-building organisations working here.

That, I thought to myself, encapsulated so much of the way we do things: a tough, security guy with a rather dark and violent past versus the wish and dream of Puff the Magic Dragon. Yet, neither could deal with the tempest of emotions and the powerful motives at play. The answers could not be 'invented,' as per the wishes of the magical singers, nor 'imposed' through security by men like Jibril Rajoub – or the Israelis who had put him in jail. The 'life is tough' approach only bred further violence, while, without more knowledge, well-meaning efforts could not penetrate the toughness and intensity in conflicts - the good feelings often dissipated as soon as the song was over. Neither could deal with that fixated and highly emotional mind that I had seen at play.

Jibril and Puff had created an epiphanic moment where clarity descends like a cool breeze. Right in front of my eyes, I saw what would not work: the storm of caprices was too strong.

ADVENTURES ON A BLUE LINE

BY 2000, I had left the Canadian Government and joined the United Nations where our job was to keep the Blue Line, the effective border between Israel and Lebanon, from lighting up. There, and elsewhere in my work in the region, I witnessed the consequences of blind, emotional overdrive. But, there were also pleasant and enlightening experiences.

As a UN official, I was allowed to cross the Lebanese-Israeli border twice to travel between Beirut and Jerusalem which was, in some ways, the natural extension of my travels along the Lebanese coast - just one step further. But also, interestingly, it was a trip through my family history. My mother and my paternal grandmother come from adjacent lands, southern Lebanon and Galilee, really one land carved by a border that I was then able to cross with something quite suitably called *the United Nations*. During this drive, I would pass the graves of all my grandparents, my grandmother Nabiha in Beit Meri, in the hills above Beirut, Azar in Saida, and Robert and Emily in Haifa.

It was also a unique opportunity to glimpse the more organic reality of the region. All in all, the trip would take about eight hours and it taught me something about the two cities that I travelled between: Beirut and Jerusalem belonged together.

Beirut is sexy, vibrant, pretentious, caressed by sea breezes. It is a city of Mercedes cars and Cohiba cigars, sophisticated restaurants, and a cosmopolitanism that speaks of Babylon, and chaos; it is a place for food and fun, a city to drive and dance in – and get very tense in.[1]

Jerusalem, on the other hand, is elegant with its pink and golden stone and cypresses and the scent of fresh rosemary. It is quiet and inspiring, embraced by a cool mountain breeze and a clear light. Yet it is also oppressive in its cultish heaviness, the worship of rocky monuments, temples and the strange ritual gear. It is a city to walk and converse in – and get very tense in.

In these two extremes, the very nature of the Middle East is expressed. A worldly cunning where all can be bought, the give and take of the bazaar, and a delectable enjoyment of food, talk and smoke. A sense of spirituality and seeming profundity, of magnetism, the land of prophets, ideals and transcendence, of a grace embodied in the hills of the Holy Land – but also of overreach and self-obsession. It seemed to me that the two cities belonged together because they complement and complete one another. Between them, there was balance; the worldly and the godly could dialogue and be enriched. But they were not the least bit linked up. Their separation was an anomaly due to the political developments of the 20th century. I don't know anyone in the region who does not dream of being able to drive from Aleppo to Gaza, or from Beirut to Jerusalem; however, the reality is something altogether different.

The Middle East is defined by cuts and divisions rather than by connection. This fragmentation is the result of agendas so narrow that they did not give a damn about the neighbours, nor any larger context. One amusing case of division and rupture was right on that Blue Line between Israel and Lebanon.

My job at the UN took me to a hilltop there, with a panoramic view of the Israeli panhandle, a site Muslims had named Sheikh Abbad, after a Sufi saint they believe is buried there. According to tradition, he was a hermit who lived 500 years ago and had followers who were makers of mattresses. In the inevitable sedimentation of history, the Israelis believe Rabbi Ashi, a Jewish sage who lived 1,600 years ago, was interred in the same place.

In 1978, in one of its first forays into southern Lebanon, Israel gained control of Sheikh Abbad hill. When Israel withdrew, 22 years later, the UN was left with the dubious task of drawing a 'line of withdrawal' between the two countries. The UN cartographers used sophisticated GPS systems to mirror the border that existed between British Mandate Palestine and French Mandate Lebanon in the early 20th century, and it came up with that 'Blue Line.'

But modern technology was accurate to within a few metres – and it passed right through the tomb of Ashi and Sufi, leaving the mini-shrine half in Lebanon and half in Israel, each receiving half a square meter of holiness. Israel had put a plaque in Hebrew to commemorate the presence of the rabbi, and the Lebanese duly scratched out the Hebrew words on their half of the shrine.

After Israel withdrew, Hizballah, the Lebanese Shia group that had fought the Israeli occupation, sent busloads of followers to visit the site. Young Lebanese would spit and throw rocks at their enemy across the line. As a consequence, the Israelis put a fence *over* the tomb, Solomonically cutting it in half. No one knows who, if anyone, lies at rest there. As one Syrian diplomat told me, "It's probably a Christian monk in there…"

Such cuts and divisions are common throughout the region. There are more famous cases, such as the Tomb of the Patriarchs in Hebron, and the Haram Al Sharif/Temple Mount in Jerusalem, holy to both Muslims and Jews. Both are contested or divided with even greater political consequences. Gaza is also fenced in, a fence/wall exists between Israel and the West Bank, and walls are up in Baghdad. Below ground, tunnelling is also popular. Hizballah has tunnels going from southern Lebanon into Israel, and right-wing Jewish settler groups are digging between the City of David and the Dung Gate of the Old City of Jerusalem.

This is not the story of the connection I experienced between Beirut and Jerusalem. I had discovered a conflicted geography where, through walls, borders, and fiery ideologies, groups, even whole nations, are trying to shape the region according to their *own* mind with little, if any, consideration of others. The consequences of ignoring context in favour of a narrow view are many. As a result of these fixations, the region today is worse off than it was 20 to 30 years ago, and war and conflict have descended upon Lebanon, Syria, Iraq, Yemen, and Libya, and many other nations are also threatened by chaos and poor governance.

In 2002, the UN Arab Development report pointed out major deficiencies in economics, education and social development in Arab countries. In 2016, after five years of Arab unrest, a new version of the study came out. In the intervening 14 years, the number of Arab countries in conflict had gone from five to eleven. With only five percent of the world's population, the Arab World was responsible for "45 percent of the world's terrorism, 68 percent of its battle-related deaths, 47 percent of its internally displaced and 58 percent of its refugees" – basically, half the world's problems.[2]

And, new problems were coming. In Yemen, 13 million people, or half the population, do not have enough clean water to drink. Most people buy water from trucks; few are connected to the unreliable municipal water supply, although that is the cheaper source. There are girls who never get an education because they spend all their days fetching water.[3] Some believe

Sanaa will become the first capital in the world to run out of that rather precious resource.[4]

Sometimes the problems are not even about lack, but about abusing what we have. When I lived in Cairo, I would pass by Lake Mariout on my way to Alexandria. An eerie pink mercurial glow hovered above its waters, making it look radioactive and other-worldly. What was once a lake of reeds for ancient Egyptians, for lovers in papyrus barks to float in, is now a pool of glowing neon. Who knows what chemicals have been dumped there, into nature's belly? Coastal cities, such as Sidon, Tyre and Tripoli, pour endless currents of raw sewage into the sea, and E. Coli levels around the Ramleh beach in Beirut are over 100 times the acceptable quality level.[5]

Despite the effort of thousands of international specialists and some of the best talent on the planet, the future of the Middle East was to be misery and drawing new mischief on. While diplomats met in fine European hotels, and leaders slept at the wheel or robbed the treasury, public services fell apart, and mafia-style economics and politics took over. The place I had left in 1968 had descended into a literal hell.

IRAQ THE SPLENDIFEROUS

IT WAS from Iraq that the darkest manifestation of this messy context was to arise. In the summer of 2014 the Islamic State in Iraq and Es-Sham (the Levant), better known as ISIS, came almost out of nowhere to seize large swathes of territory, destroy ancient heritage, and terrify millions. Their degree of savagery was shocking even for a region sadly inured to violence. Their dress conjured images of the SS merged with an oriental medieval cult, and their behaviour was like that of the Mongols of 1258, without *any* cultural background. They seemed a pure expression of evil; darkly they dressed, and dark they were.

An article published in April 2015 in the German news magazine *Der Spiegel* helps explain what methods of manipulation ISIS used to implement its scheme. It relates to the files left behind by one Haji Bakr, an Iraqi Baathist intelligence officer who went on to become one of the founders of the group:

"Bakr took up residence in an inconspicuous house in Tal Rifaat, north of Aleppo. The town was a good choice. In the 1980s, many of its residents had gone to work in the Gulf nations, especially Saudi Arabia. When they returned, some brought along radical convictions and contacts. In 2013, Tal Rifaat would become ISIS's stronghold in Aleppo Province, with hundreds of fighters stationed there...

"It was there that the 'Lord of the Shadows,' (alias Haji Bakr) as some called him, sketched out the structure of the Islamic State. ... This blueprint was implemented with astonishing accuracy in the ensuing months. ...

"The Da'wah offices [of ISIS] that were opened in many towns in northern Syria in the spring of 2013 were innocent-looking missionary offices, not unlike the ones that Islamic charities have opened worldwide. When a Da'wah office opened in Raqqa, all they said was that they were 'brothers,' and they never said a word about the 'Islamic State'...

"These offices slowly developed a network of spies and they were told to note such details as whether someone was a criminal or a homosexual, or was involved in a secret affair, so as to have ammunition for blackmailing later...

"The agents were supposed to function as seismic signal waves, sent out to track down the tiniest cracks, as well as age-old faults within the deep layers of society – in short, any information that could be used to divide and subjugate the local population...

"True to Haji Bakr's plan, the infiltration phase was followed by the elimination of every person who might be a potential leader or opponent. The first person hit was the head of the city council, kidnapped in mid-May 2013 by masked men. The next person to disappear was the brother of a prominent novelist.

"Two days later, a man who had led a group that painted a revolutionary flag on the city walls vanished. 'We had an idea who kidnapped him,' one of his friends explains, 'but no one dared any longer to do anything.' ... The system of fear began to take hold ... The goal is to deceive all but those who love God."[1]

This real-life tale of deception and manipulation is eerily similar to the story of The Demon and The Happy Couple at the beginning of this chapter. Subterfuge, lies, and illusions begot distrust and violence, one thing led to another and, all of a sudden, everyone is dead.

THE MISSING PIECE

Government remains the paramount field of unwisdom because it is there that men seek power over others - and lose it over themselves.

– Barbara Tuchman, "An Inquiry into the Persistence of Unwisdom in Government" [1]

THE PURSUIT of our own agenda at the expense of all others is, tragically, the story of much of the politics of the Middle East. In the grab of a tomb, claims on holy sites, ravaged cities, and obstacles to peace deals, each party can only see "I, me, mine."[2]

The definition of the ego in psychology is the part of a person's mind that mediates between our hidden desires and the demands of the real world. I wish we were talking about that. Instead, I am referring to something more basic, "your idea or opinion of yourself, especially your feeling of your own importance or ability."[3] In that sense, ego is not far from self-esteem or self-image, the latter being how the ego understands itself - rightly or wrongly. Most importantly this is not a light affair, we will kill and die for it. As the quote at the beginning of Part I indicates, we will indeed put aside self-preservation for our self-image.

Indeed, many of our political problems are about how we are perceived, and understand ourselves, and whether key drives and motivations are being satisfied or not. During the Ukraine and Crimea crises in 2014, the glory of the Russian people was personified by Vladimir Putin. Crimea was to become Russian again, and Eastern Ukraine devastated, and the Russian people's self-image is raised, one step up further away from humiliation. When oil prices slip, a hard economic reality hits, and yet, self-preservation still takes a second place to self-image. Europeans felt the same. "Europe must be ready to respond vigorously to further destabilisation in Ukraine and elsewhere if this is what Mr. Putin chooses, if only for the sake of our own *self-respect*." [4] National pride and honour come first. Indeed, it is the reason why economic sanctions alone don't manage to convince countries to change their behaviour.

There are obvious ways the ego plays out in politics (a leader striding the stage, or a country pursuing supremacy over others), but it is in fact such a pervasive trend that it is reminiscent of the story of the crab that sat on a rock in the ocean to tell fish about his adventures when he left the water to explore an island. As the fishes gathered around him, he eloquently explained about how different life on dry land was compared to their life in water. After giving a vivid description of the wonders he experienced on his travels he asked the fishes if they had any questions. "Yes," they said, "What is water?"

We don't often reflect on the presence of our political self-obsessions, and it can be as simple as status seeking among courtiers and analysts, political opinion, the conspiracy mind, or even an ego wrapped in apparent virtue - while the road to hell is often paved with good intentions.

For the sake of illustration, here are a few examples of the more subtle types that I have encountered in my work in international relations:

The Map Masters

She is highly educated and intelligent with a powerful abstract mind, and is very good at structuring and categorizing issues. She is working on the Middle East, has studied Arabic there briefly, but has never been immersed in the culture, does not understand the psychology of the people of the region, nor bothers to try.

She has begun work on mediation processes in the region but has never asked one question about the Middle East – nor is that curious about it. This is because her powerful mind has already come up with the pre-packaged answers, developed in Western academia, and through her own emotional and cognitive biases.

A good dose of ego makes sure that there is no need to learn whether her ideas fit in the region and its complexity; she already knows. What is important is to impose her map on the world, for it is good.

"Let's set up a meeting"

He is hyper-active and a real people person. Clever and able to say what he needs to in order to keep people engaged, his goal is to have meetings, the higher up the better. What is said in those meetings is not so important, in fact it is often ignored or developed on the hoof, because what matters is… the meeting, and the attention and status that come with it. These individuals often have a dose of ADD because they've trained their mind to flip like butterflies from flower to flower – and, in their minds, they are a beautiful butterfly indeed. What matters most is that they are seen and heard. So, in the status filled world, they often demand the stage, to give their view, even if there may not be much to say at all.

Bias

This is one of the most subtle forms of ego around. He or she prefers one country in the Middle East, and believes that it is hard done by. This is quite often Iran or Israel, and their view of the Middle East stems from that standpoint forward. How all this developed can be a grand mystery. It can be a deep anti-Americanism, or an anti-Islamism, but it is certainly not a comprehensive perspective on the region and its dynamics. These viewpoints can be close to immovable because they are a deep-seated opinion and bias, an amalgam of the personal and ideological that requires a concerted effort to change. It is a personal viewpoint that takes significant precedence over the goings-on of the world and the region.

These more subtle forms of ego activity can do as much damage in the aggregate as the blunter and more obvious variety, but we tend to ignore them, especially if they involve ourselves.

The intangible and more emotional factor in politics, the missing piece, plays out everywhere:

In 2002, as Israeli tanks rolled into Jenin killing Palestinians and leveling homes, a Jewish lawyer yelled at me at a cocktail party in Toronto, "It's the Holocaust all over again! They're trying to kill us all!" I stared at him: Israel had overwhelming power and it was the Palestinians who were being killed in Jenin.

The (self) image of fear and victimization can justify a host of Israeli actions, and the need for unrivalled power.

Anyone feeling a sense of humiliation, or a besmirched self-image, will strike. In Sierra Leone, in the early 1990s, young men from shanty towns took over power, confiscated all the "official Mercedes, Volvos and BMWs, and wilfully wrecked them on the road."[5] One of the coup leaders, Solomon Anthony Joseph Musa shot the people who had paid for his schooling, "in order to erase the humiliation and mitigate the power his middle-class sponsors had over him."[6]

In the Philippines, after the major typhoon 'Haiyan,' looters sacked department stores, but they did not steal food nor basic goods. Instead, they went after items that would provide them with status (not self-preservation): electronics, running shoes and other such items. The looters felt they had the right to take from 'the rich' and show that they are equally deserving of an iPhone or Adidas running shoes – even by thievery. Nice sneakers, better self-image.

In 2015, in Greece, we saw a government manipulate the Greek public into voting 'no' to a European austerity package because it made Greeks feel proud. Whether that was good or bad for Greece took a far second place to national pride. No matter the nationality – American, Israeli, Ghanaian – we are still run by basic instincts. 9/11 and other crises have clearly revealed the raw and often primitive emotions that lie beneath our civilized veneer and that course through our technological systems, and flood ideology. The US, once a beacon of a more open and free society, reacts impulsively. A powerful 'dragon's tail' lashes out and swats many innocent people in the process: Americans invaded Afghanistan and Iraq in short order, and without much of a plan. Instincts don't operate through plans, they just...operate – a bit like certain American presidents. In all these cases, as in many situations in the Middle East, a sense of victimhood, injustice, trauma and humiliation is driving the behaviour.

We are more of a political animal, running on reflex and conditioning, than we realize. The desire to expand or redress self-image can lead to an unchecked search for power because people believe it will help them satisfy a hunger. This can be a predatory act, or a victim aiming to be rid of oppression or seeking vengeance, i.e. to replace his or her impotence with power.

Although it is perfectly natural to fight to be rid of oppression, the consequent need for supremacy and vengeance may be where the use of power gets out of hand completely. If we are going to have fewer victims in the future and diminish the cycles of dominate or be dominated, then we need to better understand this maligned force.

Understanding the needs of the ego, managing and satisfying them would seem imperative in order to avoid or resolve conflict: **When the desires of the ego diminish, whether to feed the predator's feast or the victim's vengeance, the desire for power as an end in itself will also lessen.** The troubles in the Middle East taught me the need to take the next step in our evolution, or perish.

Working in a context such as the Middle East, and with an instinct for human foibles and obsessions, I too was aware of the shenanigans around power and prestige, and the demands of our baser self, of the political animal. I enjoyed working on the region because it involved the 'bite' of *Game of Thrones*. The difference between me and your average peacemaker is that I think there is no way to master this other than *through* our nature, soberly and step by step, other than by indulging in high-minded dialogue – or remaining in a dangerous ignorance: excessive self-interest and narrow mindsets inevitably create conflict.

However, such a focus on human behaviour and psychology in politics is often the furthest thing from people's minds. Most people continue to believe politics is about power and that's the end of that. Indeed, some might even go one step further and say there is no success in politics without the ego and its follies. "The (Jewish) settlers argued from the very beginning, Zionism flew in the face of reality. It succeeded, they said, *precisely because it ignores reality*...the demographic and geographic arguments used against settlers evaporated in the fervor of their fantasies."[7]

This book is an investigation of this factor behind endless political conflict and chaos. It is a tale of those uncontrolled emotions and drives that we barely understand, lurking beneath the surface, yet driving us on to kingdom come.

In the action-filled world of politics, such a more reflective approach sometimes draws yawns. Yet, it is also a more radical approach that goes to the heart of the problem and looks at its constituents in order to get a better hold of it.

It focuses on both individual and group dynamics, leaders and citizens, because politics inevitably involve all these elements.

Its premise is that we can evolve, and, in order to do so, tame our animal spirits, as both individuals and groups. It is also about how we can become masters of our ego in order to rule ourselves, and, ultimately, not be ruled. The admission ticket is, however, that we recognize that we are all involved.

A wise Russian once told me, "In the Middle East, if you kill a mosquito, you get a cockroach, and if you kill a cockroach, you end up with a scorpion." It might be time for a change of analogy, away from insects, to the missing piece in the equation, the human being, with all his or her warts and splendour. What follows is possibly annoyingly focused on the human being, and those very aspects of our nature that are often, incredibly, ignored when we engage in politics. The reason why is very simple. As long as we are focused on ourselves rather than the task at hand, we can never be of true service.

PART II

THE HIDDEN DIMENSION

The conscious devil is useful; the unconscious devil is perilous.

– Walter Wink, *Collected Readings* [1]

FOUNDATION STONES

Contrary to social and political science that says humans are rational, we are deeply emotional beings. … There is something deeply powerful about knowing that it's not just about culture and race ethnicity — that those things sit on an operating system called the human brain, and that that is universal.

– Michelle Boorstein, "How neuroscience is offering hope for a more peaceful world" [1]

IN MADRID, in 2015, I was present at a restaurant in Spain when the following conversation between five people working in international relations took place.

First individual (who worked in Khartoum): "What is the root cause of these young men joining ISIS? I know a young Sudanese man, well educated, from a good family, who had gone away to work as an engineer. He made enough money to send back to his family and he was getting ready to get married when he suddenly joined an extremist group. What would cause him to do this when so many things were going well in his life?"

Second: "It's these virtual communities; they're on the internet all the time; they find groups that are attractive and that give them a sense of belonging that they don't have in normal life."

Third: "I think it's also sometimes lack of sex. There are no channels for normal intimate relationships in their lives. Someone like that is going to get all heated up and those energies can be redirected."

Fourth: "In some cases, it may be a sense of alienation, being away from your culture, disconnected in a new world, like some Muslims in Europe. This will make you easy prey for someone delivering exciting messages, good feelings, and the chance to have a more meaningful life."

First again: "It's all very emotional and confusing."

In international relations, the primary focus is the management of state interests, and material concerns. These are considered hard facts, objectives that can be defined, managed and negotiated. Behind this approach is a 'homo economicus' assumption about human behaviour – the idea that we are primarily rational decision-making creatures. However, as many scientists have demonstrated recently, nothing could be further from the truth. Homo economicus, politicus or diplomaticus (i.e. rational) are all myths, as elusive as a platypus, and not the best premise for a theory of human behaviour. Diplomats are not well trained to deal with the emotional component in politics – "it's all so confusing," although some have an instinctive talent for it.[2]

Answers often come from coincidence and unexpected sources. In the summer of 2005, I was in the parking lot of the Hebrew University hospital in Jerusalem, waiting for a cousin to finish some tests (Palestinian, for those who are curious). I got out of the car to gaze across the Judean desert. The soft beige hills slipped into the Jordan Valley below, a rolling tide of rock and sand plunging into a dead horizon: space. My mind was

whirling. I had just finished reading a book called *Human Givens
– a new approach to emotional health and clear thinking* by two
psychotherapists, one Irish, one British, Joe Griffin and Ivan
Tyrrell.[3] The book provided a framework for the development of
wellbeing and understanding human behaviour: we have innate
physical and emotional needs and innate resources to help us
meet them. They called these needs and capacities, 'human
givens', because we are born with them – they are innate. Simple
enough, and I valued simple. I had always suspected that a new
direction required a back-to-basics approach, which was one
reason that smart and sophisticated people, who generally popu-
late international relations, may simply dismiss it. However,
there on the edge of the desert, I realized that it was not enough
to talk about terms like ego or self-image, and that we needed
more basic ingredients to understand our motives and
behaviour.

Griffin and Tyrrell did us the favour of identifying clearly
and comprehensively these drivers – the full set pinned down
like a butterfly in a collection for all to see:

• ***Security*** – safe territory, an environment that enables us to
lead our lives without experiencing excessive or undue fear and
that allows us to develop fully. Feeling safe!

• ***Autonomy*** – a sense of having a degree of control over
what happens around and to us, together with the flexibility of
mind to realize we can't control everything and therefore must
also develop adaptability. Some control over life.

• ***Attention*** – receiving it from others but also giving it:
good quality, balanced, attention exchange fuels the development of each individual, family and culture. Too much attention
or too little is harmful. We all need it – just look around at a
party or social function, from the attention hogs to those who
are miserable because they are incapable of eliciting it.

- ***Emotional connection to others*** – friendship, close relationships, intimacy. 'LOVE.'
- ***Connection to the wider community*** – being part of social groupings beyond our immediate family (we are social animals).
- ***Status and legitimacy*** – a sense that we are accepted, respected and valued by at least some of the various social groups we belong to, i.e. almost everything that drives politicians everywhere...
- ***Privacy*** – time and space enough to quietly reflect on and consolidate our experiences (I always needed this, but I wonder if others do, or know enough that they do).
- ***Competence and achievement*** – using our minds and bodies to our best ability, which naturally ensures a healthy level of self-confidence.
- ***Meaning*** – which comes from being stretched in what we do and how we think. Meaning makes suffering tolerable. It is through 'stretching' ourselves mentally or physically – by service to others, learning new mental or physical skills, or being connected to ideas or philosophies bigger than ourselves – that our lives feel purposeful and full of meaning.

If emotional needs are met, Griffin and Tyrrell explained, and we use our innate capacities properly, it is impossible to be mentally unhealthy, like taking in a balanced diet with the right vitamins is a precursor for health. This is a rather bold statement, but decades of health and social psychology research have demonstrated that the meeting of our emotional needs are as important to our wellbeing as the meeting of our physical needs. Needs met = health; unmet needs = illness.[4]

In my view, these powerful drivers were behind the ego's actions that I had seen in the Middle East, and that had led me to feel that Oslo would fail. We can understand this as a hidden but powerful dimension, forces seeking to be met – otherwise we are wanting, ill, anxious and desperate. When any of these innate needs are dissatisfied, or too hungry, then we will become fixated, unable to see beyond our own nose.

They are the very alphabet of the language of human motivations and group identity and we either deal with these emotions, or pay a heavy price. One thing we can't do is ignore them, as the Ancient Roman writer Horace said, "You can drive nature out with a pitchfork... (but it will still come back in the end.).".

Leader, citizen or radical, all seek to have them fulfilled politically, whether they are exhibited as ideology, political demands or, sometimes, in conflict. We will see that the deterioration of societies due to the selfish behaviour of leaders, the blind agendas of extremists, or the intractable conflict over possession of sites and land all link back to an abuse of this apparently hidden dimension.

How much status and attention does a politician need and when does his behaviour become excessive in that regard? How is a citizen's need for belonging satisfied in terms of nationalism or patriotism? To what degree do all the 'opinionators' on social media control their desire for attention while posting?

As much as hunger for food or thirst for water, these human givens need to be faced and managed successfully. The problem of course is that we also set up fantastical expectations about our needs, ones that can never be met in the real world. Unrecognized, or hijacked by manipulators, they make great fodder for political catastrophe because our appetites and their manifestation can be infinite.

In that light, we can learn from some of the most egregious ego-manipulators in the world and answer the Spanish diplomats' questions by looking at how ISIS and these human needs relate.

THE POWER OF MEETING
NEEDS IN POLITICS

I lived each day in a heightened state of alertness. Everything I did, however trivial, could seem meaningful.

– Former IRA member reminiscing about his time with the organization.[1]

I WOKE UP from a sleepless night in a hotel in Lausanne to find out that a crazed young man, apparently supported by ISIS, had exploded a bomb among young teenagers in Manchester. It was an horrific act – and it had also followed equivalent events in Paris, Nice, Berlin, Westminster, Stockholm as well as Beirut, Yemen, Cairo, Istanbul, Djakarta and forgotten towns in Iraq and Syria.

In its heyday, ISIS members believed that in a thousand years from now people would still be talking about those who built the great caliphate.[2] Some of the fighters even imagined that the World Cup would be held in Raqqa, Syria, part of their newly conquered territory. In 2014, twice as many British Muslims travelled to Syria and Iraq to join ISIS and other such groups than had joined the British military over the previous three years.[3] A dark and violent group became a success, even if only temporarily. How did this happen?

Journalist Jurgen Todenhoefer spent time with ISIS in Iraq and Syria. He discovered that, "when we stayed at their recruitment house, there were 50 new fighters who came every day. And I just could not believe the glow in their eyes. They felt like they were coming to a promised land, like they were fighting for the right thing... These are not stupid people. One of the people we met had just finished his law degree; he had great job offers, but he turned them down to go and fight... We met fighters from Europe and the United States. One of them was from New Jersey. Can you imagine a man from New Jersey traveling to fight for the Islamic State?"[4]

In Minnesota, a young Somali–American, Abdirizak Mohamed Warsame, was living a good life; he was involved in his local community, and his sister and mother fought against radicalization – and yet he chose to join ISIS.[5] [6] In another case covered by the CNN news channel, Michael Delfortrie, a Belgian, also joined ISIS. He says Islam offered him the promise of purpose as well as structure for his life, strict rules and moral clarity in a world where the prevailing liberalism favoured shades of grey over black and white.

Michael, who later became Younnes, saw Islam as an upgrade from Christianity: "I can compare it with buying a computer. If you know there's a Windows 10, you're not going to go with Windows XP." As we will see, conmen unfortunately have a knack for manipulating our hidden needs, and, unsurprisingly, a conman also played a role in his life: "While working as an apprentice in a bakery in his early 20s, Delfortrie fell under the spell of a silver-tongued Svengali – a former used-car salesman who had turned his back on a life of petty crime to become a street preacher."[7]

The pattern is what the Spanish diplomat had experienced in Sudan – normal lives gone 'wild jet ski' into the extremist stratosphere, and no one can detect it because it is going on in people's minds.

Poverty and lack of economic opportunity are often touted as root causes of extremism. However, the man from Khartoum mentioned by the Spanish diplomat was an economic success. Many of the people Todenhoefer interviewed were lawyers and professionals; and Mr. Warsame in Minnesota did not have economic problems. Indeed, according to a study by Andrew Silke, programme director for terrorism studies at the University of East London in the UK, "Most Islamist extremists (violent or not) are also from upper or middle-class backgrounds and tend to be well educated."[8] This was certainly my experience in the Middle East. It was often well-educated people who felt the world needed righting in some radical way.[9]

Anthropologist Scott Atran has done extensive field studies on what fires these young men up. He has found that most foreign volunteers to violent extremist groups like ISIS are youth in transitional stages in their lives looking for *significance*. "Mr. Hitler has discovered that human beings don't only want peace and security and comfort and freedom from want. They want adventure, glory and self-sacrifice," says Atran.[10] As the former IRA member said, "I lived each day in a heightened state of alertness. Everything I did, however trivial, could seem meaningful."[11] Atran explains that "it's the upside" – adventure and glory – that drives superlative and unusual deeds, whether for good or evil. They go to martyrdom (and murder) with a sense of profound political purpose.

It has ever been thus. Since the beginning of time, shedding blood with fellow soldiers has brought men together and fueled their imagination. It is the reason Achilles and Hector resounded through the ages. Patriotic soldiers were drawn to ideals and glory only to be torn to shreds by machine gun bullets and artillery. War, conflict, death itself, can seem noble – from a distance.

In 1914, at the beginning of the First World War, stockbrokers gathered by the hundreds at the Tower of London to go to fight in Flanders.[12] In one of the first great successes of mass propaganda, the British war hero, Lord Kitchener, asked all who had the safety of empire at heart to enlist. Of course, he meant the young men. George Coppard signed up at age 16 after a rally in Croydon, saying, "This was too much for me to resist, and as if drawn by a magnet, I knew I had to enlist right away."[13]

It is also new generations that wonder why the world is corrupt and unfair, and hold hope for change. It was such young men who led the English and French revolutions in the 17th and 18th centuries. French revolutionary Georges Danton was in his early 30s when he was killed; his cohort, Maximilien Robespierre was only 36 when, in 1785 he lost his head (for having lost his head). And it was the 'sons' (and daughters) of the Middle East that led the way during the 'Arab Spring' in 2011, and continue to do so, in Algeria and Sudan, for example. Whether they are doing it for an apparently legitimate cause, such as their nation, or for a mad ideology, young people who fight have similar motivations: a dream of a better world, or patriotism that can, in extremis, involve killing and dying. Terror and war, it seems, have a dreamy DNA; joining is a *romantic* decision even if the results are far less so.[14]

Despite the current trend that gender differences don't matter, it is young men who are intrinsically vulnerable to such rushes of glory. As Joe Herbert, a professor emeritus in neuroscience at the University of Cambridge, has said of young men, "[They] are particularly liable to become fanatics. ...They readily identify with their group. They form close bonds with its other members. They are prone to follow a strong leader. This is why young males are so vulnerable ... and why they are so easily attracted by charismatic leaders or lifestyles that promise membership of restricted groups with sharply defined objectives and values. They like taking risks on behalf of their group – and they usually underestimate the danger that such risks represent."[15] These roles were developed over millions of years of evolution, young men's vim and vigour were key to help the group survive.

Like it or not, young men are built to fight, and this powerful drive can be crystallized and channelled by a strong ideology, which doesn't have to be religious extremism. Olivier Roy, an expert on political Islam, writes: "The rallying of these young people to Daech is opportunistic: yesterday they were with Al Qaeda and before yesterday, they were subcontractors of the Algerian GIA (Groupe Islamique Armé) or they were practising, from Bosnia to Afghanistan to Chechnya, their 'nomadic' individual jihad."[16] Any exciting and *meaningful* purpose will do. Between 1980 and 2003, it was the Tamil Tigers, a secular Marxist nationalist group, that held the record for largest number of suicide attacks, and many other suicide bombers were secular.[17]

It can even be a tribal ritual. In the Philippines, among the Ilongot, young men gain their honour by chopping off heads, including those of perfect strangers who have committed no crime against the tribe. The act has been explained as a way for men to direct their frictions and resentments, and is capped off with a celebratory song.[18] The Ilongo rituals may be a little extreme for our modern sensibilities, but young men's urges do need to be directed and channelled somehow.

The variety of ideological expression speaks to something more basic behind it all. The pursuit of meaning, a basic human given, may be more critical than economics in motivating people to seek out such crusades. The *form* matters but what they are getting met *through* them – the hidden dimension – is also key. The pursuit of meaning, a basic human given, may be more critical than economics in motivating people to seek out such crusades.

What drives people towards these terrible ends is that they imagine that they have found the *right* solution, or they are in an environment that encourages such behaviour. An excited young person will cling to whatever makes sense in the search for excitement and glory, or more mundanely for their needs to be met – whatever is on offer. It is indeed not 'religion'; it is the right kind of *motivation*. By consequence, if we learn to master these motives, is it not less likely that we will have ISIS recruits?

THE TRAGIC BRILLIANCE OF ISIS

IT SEEMS to be the demon who is expert at hijacking our needs to horrific ends, the unconscious devil is perilous indeed. ISIS became a force to contend with because it deals well with that missing piece in our puzzle, the basic human motivators in our life. The recruits are getting purpose and adventure as well as a host of other needs met, and, for a while, they feel like hot shots. The needs that came up in that conversation in Madrid included young people turning to extremism for a sense of *belonging* or because of lack of sex and *intimacy*; "being away from your culture, alienated and disconnected in a new world" (lack of *status* and, again, *belonging*); and the chance to have a more *meaningful* life – all Human Givens. We can look at some of them in more detail.

Belonging (or connection)*:* As Scott Atran has written, "The best predictors (of who will become an extremist) turn out to be things like who your friends are and whether you belong to some action group. In the case of the Kouachi brothers (who committed the Charlie Hebdo attack in Paris), we had the greatest bonding experience and that is prison. But it could be soccer, it could be whitewater rafting. If you want to find out who's going to fight and die, if you want to break up a particular terrorist cell, find out what they're eating and how they dress. Plots never occur in mosques: you have to be quiet in a mosque. They occur in fast food places, soccer fields, picnics and barbeques."[1]

Researcher Pieter Van Ostaeyen has also confirmed that the pull factor is "the feeling of belonging, and the fact that they were taking part in a greater project."[2] "You just needed to snap your fingers, and you had two recruits."[3] Young men join the fight because they like to hang out together.

Status and Attention: "Terrorist or aggressive acts ... can be carried out to prove a member's worth, and attract the kind of attention that seems otherwise unattainable,"[4] writes Joe Herbert. Local recruits gain a sense of status by having control over resources and people. They become feared and respected as a local authority when only yesterday they were not even on the map. In many communities, "joining a terrorist group increases the standing of a teenager or youth considerably."[5]

Intimacy: Tragically, in some cases, even intimacy can be met through the perverse promise of sexual relations. In some parts of the Middle East, entering into intimate relationships is difficult before marriage. But, in order to have such needs met through marriage, a man must amass enough cash to set up a household. In poor economic times, or in countries full of corruption, this may be difficult, leaving many without the chance to have any intimacy within the accepted standards of their society. That excess energy among the young (or old) can lead to significant frustration – or a highly overheated imagination.

There we have it, the tragic brilliance of ISIS, a whole raft of natural human needs and animal spirits hijacked into the matrix of radicalization. The group had provided a successful platform to satisfy the ego-needs of many young men, and some women. "It is not about how they think but about how they feel," says academic Marc Sageman. Group recruitment, membership retention, and inspiration are all enhanced by these actions.

Any antidote has to address these issues, or it will not work. "They want adventure, glory and self-sacrifice" and we offer them desk jobs – or no jobs at all. The elements and success of jihadi culture confirm that alternatives to radicalism will need to target emotions rather than strictly economic interests, such as the need for employment. Solutions developed by committee or by bureaucracies don't stand much of a chance against such organic and dynamic offerings.

Many have also proposed cures for extremism that involve 'moderation.' There's an endless stream of people saying, "Why don't they just see what *real* religion is; it's about peace and love." But the minds of testosterone-laden young men won't listen easily to tepid or moderate answers. If "counter-narrative messaging" – as bureaucrats call the cure – is boring, it will be in one ear, out the other – gone in a 'puff' of smoke. What is needed is an attractive, yet constructive, alternative, heroic in the right direction.[6]

Youth need to be offered the chance to dream and meet practical and constructive challenges, even on a small scale, and to do so in an independent way. It is the upside: "My homeland is the land of truth; the sons of Islam are my brothers; I do not love the Arabs of the South any more than the Arabs of the North; ... we are all one body; this is our happy creed," wrote Ahlam Al Nasr, Jihadi poetess.[7] This is a call for a form of universalism from some of the most dangerous and violent individuals on the planet.

"Dreams are ... important, but so are their earthly custodians," said anthropologists Gwynned de Looijer and Iain R. Edgar.[8] It is not just another dream that we need to offer, but a much better grasp of how the "earthly custodians" (i.e., us) operate, and how our needs are folded into extremist politics, in order to prevent the problem from developing in the first place.

"NA BA ZAR, NA BA ZOR, NA BA ZAHR"

("Not money, not force, not poison")
– Persian saying

ISIS is an extreme case, and we can also see how needs play out in more straightforward – if difficult – conflicts such as Israel-Palestine, or the problems between Iran and the USA.

For me, the Israeli-Palestinian conflict is epitomised by two individuals, a Palestinian called Amin Majaj and an Israeli named Pini Meidan-Shani. Amin, a Palestinian doctor and a real character, hailed from Jerusalem and married my mother's cousin, Betty Dagher. Pini is an Ashkenazi Jew with origins in Austria, who worked for the Mossad for decades.

Amin and Pini could not be more different, but they are somehow representative of their peoples. Amin was an ardent Palestinian nationalist of the classical variety, the type that always wore a suit and tie, and a sweater underneath during winter. He was one of the 'pur et dur,' the old Palestinian elite that included people like Haidar Abdel Shafi and Hanan Ashrawi. These were educated and honourable men and women who did not easily compromise, nor accept the PLO 'riffraff from Tunis as their leaders. He looked down on Yasser Arafat as a kind of undesirable upstart.

The first time I saw Amin in Jerusalem was in 1993 on my first visit to the city (after the pornographic car ride). As I sat in his elegant home near Herod's Gate, he told me his view of the Oslo Accords that had been announced that very day: "If someone stole your Chevrolet and came back with the steering wheel and said, this is your car back, would you accept it?" Amin was against Oslo, he was against Arafat, and he was against Israel's presence. He believed the land belonged to its original inhabitants, the Palestinians, and that was that. However, as a violinist and a lover of classical music, he also grudgingly admired the Israeli Philharmonic Orchestra.

Amin was deputy mayor of Jerusalem in June 1967 when Israel conquered the city – there was a bullet hole in his front door to mark the event.[1] He already had an illustrious career as Minister of Health of Jordan, and had met with some fame for discovering a nutritional deficiency that caused anaemia among Palestinian refugees. Amin also had a razor-sharp wit, I liked to call him an Arab Voltaire.

He did not suffer fools gladly and believed the conflict would never be resolved. I saw in him the core of the issue: the need for Palestinians to be treated with dignity or *karameh*, in Arabic. People like Amin carried that in their person and would not let circumstance, even a powerful state like Israel, overcome it.

Dignity was the heart of the matter. The Palestinians had been 'undignified' by 1948 and 1967, and the occupation that followed. They were conquered but in their minds a part of them was always undefeated. In the eyes of the international community they were like orphans, a hangover from the end of empires.[2] From violent Hamas to non-violent Amin, the Palestinian unwillingness to compromise can be walked back to this very need. Oslo was simply insufficient – my intuition at the Canadian Foreign Ministry in 1993 wasn't all wrong.

Pini's situation could not have been more different. He had worked in the *bitakhon*, the Israeli security system, since a young age. In fact, he worked for the *bitakhon* of the *bitakhon*, the Mossad. Pini liked to show off his idiomatic Lebanese, and I imagined that he had done a few interesting impersonations during his career.

He was once close to Prime Minister Ehud Barak and became involved in the Taba peace talks with the Palestinians in 2000. I met him when working on a solution for the Old City of Jerusalem, and he believed that only a third party 'special regime', that excluded Israeli and Palestinian control, would work in the Old City. In fact, Pini was a zealot for the role of a third party in all aspects of relations with the Arabs; he wanted the involvement of others to provide guarantees and deliver what Israel needed most: security.

Pini's security mania, which is common in Israel, was such that he had reformulated the internationally accepted 'land for peace' formula, the exchange of land occupied for Israel in 1967 for peace, into 'land for security.' Israel would give up land in return for security; that was all that he really cared about: the road to peace was through security.

Words like 'peace' meant little to Pini. That was an abstraction that a practical guy like him casually cast aside. Security on the other hand – that meant everything. It is not just because Pini had worked for the Mossad that he thought like this. To a large degree, Jews were in Israel because of security, or more accurately, insecurity, forged by centuries of anti-Semitism in Europe that had culminated in the Holocaust.

Pini never veered from these basic ideas. He was an arch-realist, a 'man of gut' who called things for what they were. He also had an ability to get along with Arabs. If his need for security was provided for, he could go a long way towards compromise. He often dismissed Western attitudes towards Middle East politics because they did not understand the more basic and intangible elements of the conflict.

Pini and Amin represent core concepts, deep emotions and motives in both peoples that need to be dealt with before there is any *real* movement in finding a political solution for both sides. Because they are alive and powerful – key elements of the ego, self-image and the need for survival – these emotions can become non-negotiable if they spike or become chronically agitated. These hard-core needs require redress, or they turn into a fight.

In 2015, Iran and the USA and other big powers cut a deal on the Islamic Republic's nuclear programme. Iran and the US had been at odds for over three decades, with little exposure to each other, creating large gulfs of misunderstanding, often a breeding ground for conflict.

Well before the nuclear deal, in an opinion column in the *New York Times* on January 3, 2013, two Iranians familiar with the file, Seyed Hossein Mousavian and Mohammad Ali Shabani, suggested a way to bridge the gulf.[3] They clarified two simple concepts in Iranian culture: *maslahat* and *aberu*.

Putting it simply, *maslahat* is interest, which traditionally drives state policy and negotiations. *Aberu* is 'saving face,' or dignity, reflecting the need for status and legitimacy and a sense of belonging to a wider social community (in this case the international community) – two basic needs that have to be met before any progress can be made.

The authors made a clear argument that Iran will never put *maslahat* before *aberu*, or interest before dignity. In other words, they recommended that emotional needs be addressed <u>first</u>. "If there is to be any resolution of the nuclear standoff, Western leaders must grasp these concepts," they said.[4]

Iran is an ancient civilization and culture. It has a pride and honour in that history, which translates into a demand to be treated with a certain respect, and this can be at the cost of physical self-preservation. Iran is also a tricky and highly sophisticated actor on the international stage, and, of course, this complicates things.

Originally, decision makers in the US gave short shrift to the ideas that these authors proposed. Indeed, the "cornerstone of the West's strategy … has always been to contain and punish (Iran)."[5] Their aim was to ensure that Iran's leaders faced "a stark choice between holding on to their nuclear program or reviving the oil revenue, the country's economic lifeblood (*maslahat*)."[6] In other words they maintained a focus on material interest, and on the use of threat, to make the enemy bow down in defeat. And, of course, it completely ignored the Iranian need for status and legitimacy. "Placing *maslahat* over *aberu*, even temporarily, leads to nothing good… Western leaders need to grasp that it would be devastating for Iran's *aberu* to take the first step solely in exchange of promises," wrote Mousavian and Shabani.[7] The Iranians needed to have their status and sense of belonging internationally recognized *first*.

In the final accord, Iran provided the West with full transparency into its nuclear programme, permitting inspections to determine whether Iran was attempting to build a bomb, in return for a recognition of its right to enrich uranium, and a removal of economic sanctions. How is this related to emotional needs? The right to enrich uranium is seen by Iran as the prime indicator of its status and belonging in the international community. It does not want to be treated differently from other nations who have that right.[8]

The Americans had their own need for status, with regard to Iran, as well as an unmet need for security. Americans have not forgotten the 1979–80 hostage crisis in Iran, nor the bombings of the American embassy and the Marine compound in Beirut by Iranian-related groups, nor attacks on American soldiers in Iraq abetted by Iran. These actions naturally led Americans to perceive Iran as a threat to their security, and made the superpower feel humiliated (reduced status) by a lesser power.

Both nations had basic unmet emotional needs that were playing havoc with their capacity to pursue more rational talks and successfully conclude complex negotiations. Time and time again, each side had sought to have their basic needs met in an improper or ineffective fashion. Unmet needs lead to frustration, and manipulation to get them met – and from there an inability to think and act constructively. However, "na ba zar, na ba zor, na ba zahr" ("not money, not force, not poison"), no form of coercion, worked on its own.

For Iran, the desire for status, legitimacy and attention, buttressed by an imperial history, drove it to pursue tactics, including ambiguity in the nuclear programme and loud and threatening rhetoric, that were perceived internationally as pernicious and untrustworthy. For the Americans, the need to maintain status as an unrivalled superpower was translated into a refusal to compromise with a party that was attempting to be on equal footing with the US, and that had done it damage. These drivers, combined with the political habits and cultures of each side, resulted in destructive and confrontational policies that only make sense to people *within* each society.

In the end, the deal came about once the negotiators and, importantly, the leaders, attended to the *aberu* component. The two presidents, Barack Obama and Hassan Rouhani, saw the need to manage this factor deftly, while simultaneously managing backlash within their respective societies.

Of course, other factors are at play and cannot be ignored. Iran's regional behaviour was not negotiated in the accord because the American administration assessed that it would be too much for the market to bear. As a result, some view the deal as having provided Iran with a carte blanche for continued interference in many Arab states – and they are not wrong. The Obama administration, by effectively ignoring or mismanaging its allies, the Gulf countries, also left a stew of unmet needs there. Today, we see the consequences of that decision.[9]

Some also believe that the economic sanctions were key to bringing Iran to the table. Indeed, Iranians were feeling the pinch due to sanctions; however, the Mousavian–Shabani factor needed to be addressed in order for the negotiations to *succeed*. Sanctions alone could not do it. They were part of the overall process but not the key ingredient to set the stage for a deal. Even later, when US President Donald Trump used economic sanctions to try to force Iran into submission, Samuel Menassa, a Lebanese journalist and a keen observer of the Middle East told me, "The West just doesn't get it, they will never fold because of financial or economic pressure. That's just not how the East works..."

Aberu was the missing piece of the equation, a more human way for the two sides to deal with each other, and an example of what we can call 'mutual needs satisfaction' – a term that will be particularly useful as we move forward. The lesson is there for anyone who wishes to be constructive to draw on: deal with the powerful elements of the ego first.

DEALING WITH PRIMARY CAUSES

ONCE UPON a time there was country with countless doctors attending to all sorts of matters. But, every year, the citizens kept dying at a younger and younger age. What was the answer to this tragic circumstance? Why, more doctors of course. However, the lifespans of the people kept shrinking, and every year they died at a younger and younger age.

What nobody had yet introduced was the idea of invisible things, microbes, that were the very cause of the tragic deaths of the citizens in this land of many doctors.

It is not simply an increase in the number of mediators, analysts, politicians, diplomats, and intelligence officers that will get results in international relations (and recently, we have seen a proliferation of all of the above). Instead, we have to become aware of the real cause of our troubles.

Most people have never seen a microbe or a virus, but now they conduct their lives as if they exist. Similarly, our emotional needs are invisible yet have a mighty effect. Fortunately, a positive inoculation for emotional madness can occur if greater knowledge about ourselves spreads, serving as a kind of immunization to our ignorance.

We are at a stage where we don't need more doctors; we

need more knowledge. Once we recognize that something invisible but powerful and all around us is plaguing us, then, we will begin to find a cure.

We are unused to dealing first with hidden and primary causes. Many diplomats and politicians do understand this approach, often working to respect the other side's dignity and basic needs. A bold example is when former Egyptian President Anwar Sadat went to Jerusalem to speak at the Knesset, setting a proper and solid emotional basis for the consequent negotiations. In contrast, some politicians also use these emotional forces for nefarious purposes, and politics are often a mishmash of primary, secondary, and tertiary dynamics all woven together (which is why it is so key to become aware of what *is* primary).

In that light, let's have a look at how these basic human needs translate politically:

Security:
• Israel's need for security, a la Pini.
• Any Arab citizen wishing to avoid being jailed, shelled, or oppressed by some party or another, whether their government or rival ethnic and national groups.

Autonomy:
• The Palestinian need for political independence.
• Arab youth striving to be rid of constricting authority they experience as tyranny.

Attention:
• Iran sought the attention of the USA through its dealings on the nuclear file, even through negative behaviour, as did North Korea in the crisis and talks of 2017-2018. Attention seeking is also a prime motivator

for many politicians: the question is how much is enough?

Emotional connection to others:
• The Middle East is quite good at providing this in daily social life if sometimes at the cost of emotional blackmail. However, we have also seen how lack of intimacy be also used by extremists.

Connection to the wider community:
• Israel's need to be accepted by others in the region.
• Iran's need to be part of a global system.

Status (or Legitimacy):
• Palestinians' need to feel dignified politically.
• Iran's need to have the right to enrich uranium, as other countries do.

Privacy
• In many places in the Middle East, there is very little of it. For example, in very crowded Cairo, it is a significant problem, and the mind goes haywire.

Competence and achievement
• Arab youth trying to get rid of the plug on top of their heads (the authority figures), and to have the space to pursue individual achievement.
• Organizations such as Hizballah and the Israeli army are successful because they enable this for their members.

Meaning
• ISIS provides it for its followers
• Jewish settlers in the West Bank, Muslim Brothers and

their political dreams, and 'Jerusalem' as a meaningful cause for almost everyone.

A look at the list above shows how even the bitterest of enemies share the same basic needs and motivations. There is something quite powerful in knowing that we have a common operating system and that the human givens are universal.

As Michelle Boorstein said, the bottom line is that "we are deeply emotional beings," and if our emotional needs are not met, and that self-image is not somehow satisfied, there will be trouble. *How* we get these needs met is as important as satisfying them.

PART III

THE MAGNIFIED SELF

DEATH BY IDENTITY

The biological impulse that drives men to irrational deeds.

– Lev Gumilev

MY WORK and learning, my 'search,' did not end in the Middle East, and I was fortunate to discover other lands. I visited Moscow for the first time in 2016 and it captivated me. I sensed Russia's special charm, a magical quality in the air that I had also felt in the Middle East. Despite the Americanization of the consumer streets, a facade of Zara and Zegna in the imperial capital, the sense of 'other civilization' remained strong. Moscow looked Western enough but, somehow, sitting on the edge of vast Asia, it left a sense of other possibility and undiscovered grandeur.

I also sensed that this was a dynamic culture, not yet fossilized and gridlocked by laws, regulations and the often dogmatic and uninventive dictates on speech as seen in the West today. Russians lived passion and attachment to each other, which can also sometimes translate into compassion. However, like many intense emotions, this was a force that could be misdirected; passion for one's country also means a readiness to become aggressive, and to suffer for a greater cause.[1] Intense group belonging can be a larger, more magnified, and highly satisfying form of ego.

A couple of weeks after my visit, I happened upon an article about Lev Gumilev, a 20th century Russian historian, that further demonstrated this:

"Gumilev became a renowned expert on the steppe tribes of inner Eurasia: the Scythians, the Xiongnu, the Huns, Turks, Khitai, Tanguts and Mongols. Their history did not record the progress of enlightenment and reason but rather an endless cycle of migration, conquest and genocide. Every few hundred years, nomads would sweep out of the steppes, plunder the flourishing kingdoms of Europe, the Middle East or Asia, and then vanish into history's fog just as quickly as they had come.

"The victors in these struggles were not the societies that led the world in technology, wealth and reason. Instead, they had something that Machiavelli described as virtù, or martial spirit. ... To Gumilev, this was *passionarnost* ... the biological impulse that drives men to irrational deeds...

"'There is not a single person on earth outside of an ethnos,' he was fond of saying. 'Everybody will answer the question, "What are you?" with "Russian," "French," "Persian," "Maasai," etc., without a moment's hesitation.'"

What distinguishes an ethnos from a jumble of languages, religions and historical experiences is a *common purpose*, and the willingness of members to sacrifice themselves for it.

To be fair to Gumilev, he was not devising a racially or ethnically tinged theory of nationalism, but stating only that the urge to identify with a nation is so pervasive that it must be an essential part of human nature. He concluded, "with all due respect, the West does not understand it."[2]

Gumilev's ideas are not far from those of one of the first sociologists of history, the 14th century Arab savant, Ibn Khaldoun. As one reference to him states,

"Ibn Khaldun's central concept of *asabiyyah* … has been translated as 'social cohesion', 'group solidarity', or 'tribalism'. This social cohesion arises spontaneously in tribes and other small kinship groups; it can be intensified and enlarged by a religious ideology. … This cohesion carries groups to power but contains within itself the seeds – psychological, sociological, economic, political – of the group's downfall."[3]

Gumilev and Ibn Khaldoun emphasized that social cohesion infused with passion is crucial for success in any group competition. Ibn Khaldoun adds the important idea of the possibility of 'downfall,' which Gumilev, and presumably some Russian leaders, ignore.

Again, this identity-force is not just an academic concept – it's a living, breathing, and sometimes bloody dynamic. People are ready to fight and die (and even vote for a demagogue) for it. This identity force is a powerful packaging of our basic motivations (the human givens) and a way for people to have big needs met and magnified.

We operate in groups from the family upwards, and human motivations and emotional needs are always in play since we get most of our needs met through our interactions in groups. Our needs do not sit in isolation, they blend into those of others, and most of the political experiences I had in the Middle East involved groups – extremists, nations, political parties – interacting in conflicted ways.

At a meeting in Lausanne, a group of Syrians were looking at how to build a future for their war-torn country. They were pondering the need to develop a new constitution and whether a national dialogue, a forum for discussing their differences, would be useful. An expert, who happened to be Syrian, presented the case for a national reconciliation process. He indicated that Syria was an ethnically and religiously divided country with more frictions between groups than many would care to admit.

As he discovered, most of the Syrians present did not share his view. He was set upon verbally, mostly by the older set full of nostalgia for a dreamy Syrian nationalism. They maligned him for spreading a kind of sedition. His attackers insisted that it was Assad's manipulations and outsiders that had created the hatred and violence, not identity differences between Syrians. Assad had played into minorities' worries about Sunni domination, and the French had empowered the minority Alawites during the Mandate by providing them with powerful positions. Iranians had also used fears of Sunni extremism to advance their agenda. Powerful groups and individuals do manipulate our identities. But, none of this was the fault of the Syrians who were just good nationalists, said the rest of the crowd.

The presenter became quite uncomfortable under the verbal barrage, until a young man spoke up. This fellow had been sitting sheepishly in a corner, but, after having witnessed the attack on the expert, he took the microphone and stated calmly that the presenter was right. He said that, if a sincere national dialogue and reconciliation process were not started in Syria, there would be much worse than ISIS coming in the future. If the ethnic differences and traumas were not addressed, the wound would fester, and anger would grow.

He was the only one in the room who had any experience fighting, and he had left the battlefield to work politically. "I don't care if you think I'm a terrorist. If you don't do as the expert is suggesting, there will be more violence, because Sunnis will never accept the situation as it is," he said. He was predicting some unvarnished 'death by identity,' as the Middle East experiences every day.[4]

Gumilev and Ibn Khaldoun were not intellectual slouches – combining identity and political purpose can work well. Much of Iran's regional success today is not only due to its readiness to spend money on groups that follow its agenda, nor to its considerable Persian wile, but also to its ability to inspire a Shia sense of *asabiyyah*, group identity and shared purpose to gather people from various countries to fight and die for a common Shia cause. Iran would not be able to make its regional gains without this emotional call to Shia identity. In fact, Iran's methodology is more successful than the Lebanese, Iraqi, Syrian or Yemeni states' ability to rally citizens to a national cause – and, so far, it wins.

Although identity can be 'constructed,' as some academics would suggest, it is not like raising a building; it is like unleashing a horde upon the planet, Gumilev style, whether digitally or on the steppes. An unsatisfied or besmirched sense of identity (i.e., unmet needs) can open the floodgates for the most extreme strains of this trend. Death by identity is waiting for us around the proverbial corner, unless we become more aware of how much, and how important, group identity can be.

IDENTITY MATTERS

IDENTITY POLITICS is popular these days, especially in Western academic circles. What this usually means is a conscious effort to focus on someone's specific characteristics as something to be respected and treasured, and especially those related to having been victimized by another, more powerful group.

Identity differences do not automatically translate into conflict, and today there are Sunni Arab countries, such as Egypt or Qatar, that are not in conflict with Iran. During the Shah era, Saudi Arabia and Iran did not have major differences. Jews have often lived with Muslims and Christians in the Middle East. Kurds have not always had battles with Turks.

But, this modern notion of 'identity politics' seems to me an ivory tower construction aimed at protection from the vicissitudes of life, often under the rubric of justice. Identity and group behaviour, as I refer to here, is closer to 'nature red in tooth and claw.' It's a life force, often unconscious, something that creates history, it is core to being a deeply political animal.

Today, in Yemen, Lebanon, Iraq, and Syria, there is a major battle going on between Iran and Saudi Arabia. Their rivalry is geopolitical, and the dispute is fuelled and abetted by differences of identity (one is Sunni and Arab, the other Persian and Shia). The two countries are deeply suspicious of each other and, beneath it all, their differences go back millennia, to basic covenants, loyalties and misunderstandings regarding religious origins, mingled with current concerns and interests.

For those fixated on modern times and interpretations, this has happened before. As Frederick Starr explains in *Lost Enlightenment: Central Asia's Golden Age*, "Strife within the community of Islam, the umma, the struggle of Sunni vs. Shia, was more than anything responsible for the closing of the Muslim mind in Central Asia."[1] That was in the 13th century. So, although identity is not always the cause of conflict, ignoring its role may be foolish.

Identity is not also always the invasion of countries or flag-waving patriotism, it can operate in more subtle ways. I noticed this in myself when I was having a drink with a friend at Café 27 in the Badaro district of Beirut, with "L.A. Woman" by The Doors blaring from the speakers. She was a foreigner working in Lebanon and was explaining her (valid) frustrations with the country: the huge egos, the aggressive behaviour, and the fixations on forms. I found my blood rising, wanting to correct her, to suggest that she needed to see the good *and* the bad in Lebanon – even though I completely agreed with her. *I had often said the same things myself,* yet my emotions blinded me to my own truth because it was coming from a complete foreigner.

It can even play out over one word – or one letter. Palestinians and Lebanese pronounce the Arabic word for tomato differently. During the Lebanese civil war, people would be asked at a checkpoint to pronounce it, and a wrong answer meant a wrong turn for one's life. This has happened before: "And the Gileadites took the passages of Jordan before the Ephraimites: and it was so, that when those Ephraimites which were escaped said, Let me go over; that the men of Gilead said unto him, Art thou an Ephraimite? If he said, Nay;

Then said they unto him, Say now Shibboleth: and he said

Sibboleth: for he could not frame to pronounce it right. Then they took him, and slew him at the passages of Jordan: and there fell at that time of the Ephraimites forty and two thousand."[2] Banadoura/bandora, shibboleth/sibboleth, it's a longstanding tradition.

In politics, a minor blood rise of this kind, multiplied many times over, can rapidly swell into a dangerous mass movement – as, for example, happened recently between Catalonia and the rest of Spain, when Catalans felt that the Spanish central government was not attending to their identity.

Many argue that the fight for economic resources and power is what is truly behind conflict, not identity. However, a study that looked at the use of public expenditure in the predominantly Kurdish provinces in Turkey tells us otherwise. The spending was an attempt by the central Turkish state to change voting patterns away from Kurdish independence groups towards the central government in Ankara. It was inspired by the Turkish elites' view that the Kurdish problem is driven by economic backwardness, and public spending could make the Kurds more beholden to the central state, weakening their identity ties. However, after such an attempt, these provinces shifted towards *more* support for Kurdish parties while gaining greater prosperity. The effort failed, identity won.[3]

How do we reconcile this dichotomy between geopolitics and the clash of material interests and the role of identity, and which one plays the greater role? In Libya, the case continues to be made that all the various groups, ideological, ethnic or tribal, are after the oil wealth. Do threats appear because of identity differences or is identity simply a vehicle for fighting out economic or resource competition?

Identity, at whatever level, is a mechanism that evolved to motivate individuals to group solidarity and action, and victory over the enemy. We survive and thrive through our groups, and we pursue our interests through them. Few will doubt that when threats appear, identity often becomes the device that helps the group survive, or carries it to success and power, or failure.

People are after the oil wealth not only for personal gain but to help *their* family, tribe or group; the land and oil are valuable because they are for *our* people, (the assumption being that the individual will also gain through that equation).

Identity is therefore both the means and the end of the behaviour – hence its power and its role as a driving force in all our history. It is a magnified self. As we will see, it can also be a way of pursuing a form of self-transcendence or losing ourselves in something larger.

None of this should come as a surprise given that many of our individual innate needs – the need for connection and belonging, status and meaning – are all met through this evolutionary survival package.

THE HIVE SWITCH

IN HIS BOOK, *The Righteous Mind: Why Good People are Divided by Politics and Religion,* social psychologist Jonathan Haidt provides us with a good look at what is behind our group behaviour, and he also emphasizes a more practical purpose. Social rules and norms, or 'morality,' if you wish, bind us together and are essential for our survival. Through implicit and treasured codes of conduct, our cultures evolve to ensure that we cooperate effectively within our group, or lose.

Indeed, one clear to tame our individual egos is to make them part of something larger, to join our tribe or nation in the pursuit of its goals. This automatically limits our behaviour and our individual desires. We transgress these codes only at a high social cost, for, we will have diminished our group's chances of survival. Indeed, Haidt demonstrates that self-interest is a weak predictor of policy preferences: people care *more* about their groups than their individual interest when making key choices.

"We evolved to live, trade and trust within shared moral matrices," Haidt says, and the Middle East once offered that.[1] In medieval Islamic societies, the principle of God, trust and trade was successfully applied. Islamic culture helped bind people in trust, allowing them then to trade with greater efficiency and prosperity.

But, Haidt goes beyond this clearly practical evolutionary gain. In day-to-day interactions between individuals, respect, affection, honour, fear, and maintaining reputation or self-image are the currencies at play (many of them have parallels in human givens). All of these leave the individual with his/her autonomy and personality relatively intact – they are transactional, if you wish.

However, there is a second way in which we interact, one that binds an individual to his social entity completely, where we each lose ourselves happily into a greater whole. This is the Gumilev agenda, and Haidt calls this "the hive switch," when a population acts as a single unit, ready to live and die for the group. And it really is a 'switch,' we know and can see when a herd 'switches on,' moving as a single unit.[2] The individuals involved enter another dimension, completely alien from the particular beings they were when having a casual coffee with friends.

Our groups can represent larger, more interesting forms of our individual ego, and, by entering them, we can be more fully empowered. This magnified self, or group ego, offers safety, security, and meaning, and, through the hive switch, even a form of transcendence. "Through a fixed and unique relationship with something larger and more lasting than himself (the citizen)... he has defeated the pressures of anonymity which myriad life continually brings to bear on the individual's psyche."[3] Such collective emotions can pull humans fully but temporarily into what feels like the sacred.

Haidt also stresses that these 'hives' have a normal and healthy function. When we lose ourselves in our group, we are reaching for greater purpose and we can truly feel being part of something larger, and it does provide deeper meaning.

Indeed, societies that cherish autonomy too much and encourage only the transactional interests of members (e.g.,

Canada's multiculturalism), and that lack opportunities for losing oneself in the group (beyond watching "Hockey Night in Canada"), score *lower* on social capital, mental health and happiness. Indeed, the lack of 'hive switch' explains the sense of anomie I have seen among Arab friends and relations living in Canada; they could not lose themselves in the Canadian hive, which is tepid to start with.

It may also be what I had desperately sought to regain in the fun and meaning of family and cultural belonging back in the Middle East. I pursued it so intensely that I ended up with a 25-year sentence in the emotional gulags of the region, where I learned that the identity factor was not all fun, falafel and Arabic pop songs – or positive hive switch.

The sacrifice of ourselves in the name of our nation may be one of the greatest acts of ego out there. Once we do it, once we *are in it*, we forget words and reasons. It's a grand feeling that can lead to the invasion of Russia (never a good move). However, as crucial as the hive switch is for our contentment, if it scales up too much, it becomes, effectively, a nation-cult.

As we saw in the case of human needs, Haidt also emphasizes that, contrary to what most people think, "intuitions come first; strategic reasoning comes second."[4] Our collective identities, he says, are like a rider sitting on an elephant. The 'elephant' is our intuitive/emotional impulse and motive force, and the rider is our more rational and narrative side. The rider tends to serve the elephant, not the other way around. If the elephant leans in one direction, the rider will lean with it (Maslahat/Aberu).

If the Sunni elephant in Syria is dissatisfied, it will lean and take the young man and everyone else in that room in directions that may not make sense to 'strategy' or reason. In 1967, the Israeli elephant leaned towards Jerusalem, and in 2014, the Russian mammoth towards Crimea. All the research papers in the world and the pleas on Facebook will not stop this rampage by Jonathan Haidt's "elephant," which is why it's so important to listen to that former Syrian warrior who spoke up during that meeting in Switzerland.

The problem is that if people can't satisfy their need for deep meaning through their local communities, then they may become receptive to manipulative leaders who appear to offer that deep meaning by pursuing national and potentially destructive agendas: Canada can become Russia. As I had seen in the region, elephants can be hijacked. Almost all my *political* experiences in the Middle East were just that: elephant hijacks. As Haidt says, "when a single hive is scaled up to the size of a nation and is led by a dictator, the results are invariably disastrous."[5]

'CULT U RE'
THE CULT IN CULTURE

The devious manipulation of sheep, otherwise known as politics, never caught my imagination.

– Jason Elliot, *The Madhouse* [1]

IMAGINE THAT there is a dark blue inkblot on every map appearing in every book and on every wall that you see. In the Lebanon of my youth, these patches were always in one place: where Israel was. Someone had been hired by the Lebanese government to blot Israel out of every single map in the country. This was heavy-duty censorship and I remember that the ink was often so deeply imprinted that the paper's fibres had unravelled. Someone had been using a quill or fountain pen with great vigour. Maybe he was an especially enthusiastic individual, with an accountant's eyeglasses and cheap suits; maybe he slapped on Old Spice, or happened to be a good and considerate father. Maybe he was a she.

The person who did this, however, probably thought it was good, not evil. Israel was a hated enemy, a usurper of Arab land and rights, and it was not only erased from the maps, its name was never mentioned. It was the 'Zionist entity,' as if stating its name might begin the fatal slide into acceptance. The inkblot was a grand denial of reality; the Arabs were preoccupied in their imagination, protecting plundered self-esteem, while Israel thrived.

Of course, this blindness is an equal opportunity event. Menachem Klein, an Israeli scholar and fine human being, explained to me that when Israeli settlers see the Arab village of Anata on the outskirts of Jerusalem, they see Anatot, the biblical village of Israelites, not Anata. The living, breathing Arab residents are not there, only the imagined Hebrew past. All else is just scaffolding for their imagination.

The same phenomenon is true of Jewish groups such as the Temple Mount Faithful, who want to pray on the platform where the Al Aqsa Mosque and the Dome of the Rock sit today, because it is their Temple Mount.

"Why shouldn't we come in with a young goat and offer the Passover sacrifice on the Temple Mount?"... When you are standing up there on the Mount, with these people, [religious Jews]… are…not seeing what you see. They are seeing the place of the sacrificial altar. The site of the Temple. They are in a different dimension … They're on a high … These people are seeing on the Mount a mythological past and a mythological future, and not the present."[2] The Muslim reality does not exist for them, only the goat, the sacrifice and their imagined link to the past.

The Palestinian who lost his orchard seven decades ago, ISIS recreating the caliphate, or Shia with a sense of victimization because of the memory of martyred caliph Ali – all are involved in profound and powerful imaginings that annihilate any inconvenient other reality.

Such denial can be a flight of political fancy, or become a

full-blown fantasy that leaves destruction and suffering in its wake:

- The excited love of late Egyptian President Gamal Abdel Nasser and Arab nationalism in the 1960s, without any real results for the Arabs.

- The Israeli idea that the Holy Land was empty for Zionism to pursue its agenda, with no Palestinians around.

- The possibility of Iranian-Shia hegemony over a Sunni-majority Middle East.

- Turkish policies of "zero problems with neighbours," whereas the result has been problems with almost everyone.

- Muslim Brothers' rule of an Islamic Umma from the Atlantic to the Euphrates. Gone. Poof.

In more subtle ways, this blindness also affected intelligence analysis by Israel and the USA prior to the 1973 Yom Kippur / October War. Both services had data regarding Syrian and Egyptian military build-up, but interpreted it, or more accurately dismissed it, because of 'preconceptions.' The ensuing war resulted in an existential threat to Israel and a Soviet-American confrontation.[3] As the title of the article that portrayed this failure suggests, 'why be confused by the facts?' Such diminished realism can literally kill us. It may mean missing a key factor in a crisis, or misunderstanding the enemy's motives and capacities, leaving us prone to defeat or haemorrhaging in an unnecessary war.

The inkblot did not prevent the Arab defeat of 1967 and led Israel to errors in 1973. We risk missing out on a larger context at our peril.[4]

However, in the previous section we also saw the importance and benefits of entering the group mind, so what swings it one way or another? How can we manage this deep socio-biological investment?

The term 'tribalism' is often linked to the region: 'Tribes with Flags,'[5] The 12 Tribes of Israel, the many tribes of the Arabian Desert. When you travel to the region, the comforting sense of 'tribe' is immediately evidenced in the friendliness of people. A pleasant sense of belonging pervades the air, but so does the threat of spilled blood, should the vitals of that 'tribe' be threatened.

An Afghan diplomat hit the nail on the head when he was talking about the problems in his country: "When there is tribalism, there is lack of empathy," he said. Those outside our group are perceived as less valued, and this cuts to the core of international relations, and to being human. An overactive ego, in an individual or group, and high emotion fix our minds firmly on what we need or want, and all else is forgotten. If others don't share our fixation, they will react and clash – and conflict will ensue.

This tribal mind however does not exist without culture. Every single group on the planet has some degree of culture, habits and rituals that make the individual feel like they belong. The group provides rules regarding behaviour, and that motivate them in a common direction. There may be another way of looking at this to help us manage our fate as social animals and political beings.

Arthur Deikman was a clinical professor of psychiatry at the University of California, San Francisco and he has written some important books – *Personal Freedom* and *The Observing Self* are two of my favourites.[6] He provides us with an invaluable paradigm, and explains in one word yet another way that unmet emotional needs can leave us highly vulnerable: cult.

In *Them and Us: Cult Thinking and the Terrorist Threat*, Deikman explains how cult behaviour is part and parcel of our humanity, how we all partake in it and how it affects our group mindset. It does not, as is usually believed, only involve strange robes or purple Kool-Aid drinkers in Guyana. It is far more pervasive. It can explain trouble between tribes, and even between nations. The astute doctor identified four main characteristics of cults:

1. Dependence on a leader or *obeying blindly what an authority tells us, fearing his or her judgments*

2. Avoiding dissent within the group

3. Group Compliance

4. Devaluing outsiders: "When there is tribalism, there is lack of empathy."

Importantly, this process develops naturally when we bind in groups – *any* group. This is the cost of being social animals. But it also blinds (the inkblot effect that we just looked at: 'why be confused by the facts'), and permits us to feel superior to the world outside.

Cults are vertical structures; members look upwards to an authority figure, or any symbol or object that serves that purpose, and lose the ability to look outwards. This is a pervasive tendency in Middle East politics. Authoritarianism, 'follow the leader,' involves obeying blindly without critical thought. As Voltaire said, "To learn who rules over you, simply find out who you are not allowed to criticise." Indeed, many follow a leader *because* he is top dog. I saw a Turk interviewed on television before his country's referendum of 2017, who said, "We know Erdogan is authoritarian. That's why we like him." This is dependency on a leader.

In order for the group to remain internally coherent, dissent must be diminished, and taboos arise to enforce this. Limited information is taken in, usually only whatever is congruent with the group's codes and traditions. In the Middle East, shame is often used to prevent offensive actions or words. However, in the process of maintaining taboos, lies and falsehoods can also be encouraged and spread. Dissent can be labelled as treason, and tyrants go a bit further, they imprison or kill you for it.

Possibly, most importantly, when one joins the silo of a cult, outsiders are automatically devalued. Those on the inside are superior to those on the outside and we come to see the latter as less human, taking the first step to enabling violence against them.

Jonathan Haidt claims that, in general, groupishness is focused on the welfare of the in-group, rather than on harming an out-group. In my political experience in the Middle East devaluing outsiders was pervasive, and didn't seem to be much good for anyone. The exclusion and dehumanization of the outsider was core to keeping endless cycles of revenge and conflict going, blocking movement forward: Israel/Palestine, unresolved; Syria, broken; Saudi Arabia and Iran, at each other's throats; Turkey and the Kurds, in infinite struggle, much of it because one side sees the demands of the other as basically *inferior*, and ultimately, irrelevant or invalid.

In the worst cases, outsiders are seen as a virus to be annihilated, which explains why many can enact grotesque acts against their enemy without even flinching: "They are not us, they are not even them – they are nothing," said an Israeli soldier about the Palestinians during the Intifadah of the Knives of late 2016. Mehmet Resid, a 20th century Ottoman Turkish governor, also known as the "Butcher of Diyarbekir" for his destruction of the Armenian, Assyrian and Greek communities in his region of eastern Anatolia during World War 1, regarded the Armenians as "dangerous microbes" in "the bosom of the Fatherland."[7]

The following is a description of what happened after the capture in 2017 of the city of Mosul from ISIS by Iraqi forces:

"The (Iraqi) officers did not see their victims as humans, let alone as fellow Iraqis: they were simply the enemy. They needed to hear the ISIS soldiers who had been their tormentors begging for mercy, before they could celebrate their final victory. They needed to hear the ISIS soldiers' animal squeals of pain, in order to feel they had avenged the loss of their families. Perhaps ISIS's victory lies in its conversion of the Iraqi people to its own methods."[8] Again, this is the Iraqi army, not ISIS. Very simply, cult thinking is a mental state that can ultimately facilitate killing in any of us.

Let us take a look at a living political example of cult thinking. When the Egyptians took a U-turn back to authoritarianism under General Abdel Fattah el-Sisi, they quickly established a dependency on their new leader. Meeting their need for security, under his guidance and authority, seemed preferable to meeting their need for dignity. Meanwhile, the Muslim Brotherhood government that Sisi threw out in 2013 had been itself indulging in considerable cult behaviour. Shadi Hamad, an analyst at Brookings Institute, recounts "the group's secretive decision-making process, its tendency to put organizational self-interest above nearly everything else (as well as) the authoritarian tendencies of President Morsi."[9]

Ashraf El-Sharif, a lecturer in political science at the American University in Cairo also writes: "The [Muslim Brothers were] plagued by attempting political domination, and ignoring others ... and being *incapable of adaptation.* Its rigid, hierarchical structure prevented it from successfully reacting to rapid societal changes."[10]

As a result, the Muslim Brotherhood government was blind to Sisi's plans to overthrow them (diminished realism). This was despite the fact that they had appointed him and, in their cult bubble, ignored warnings that he was plotting against them. By diminishing dissent and restricting new information, cult thinking halts the flexibility of mind required to adapt to new circumstances.

In contrast, the Tunisian Ennahda party, modelled on the Muslim Brotherhood, showed less cult-like thinking, and it survived. As scholar and researcher Vasily Kuznetsov described it, "In the sociological sense Ennahda has always been heterogeneous [less culty], which enabled it to demonstrate extraordinary ... flexibility."[11]

Another example of how cults work in politics, especially dependence on a leader, comes from a passage from an essay by Vladislav Surkov, who was once Putin's *éminence grise*: "In this new (Russian) system all institutions are subordinated to the main task: trust-based communication and interaction between the head of state and the citizens. The various branches of government come together at the person of the leader and are considered valuable not in and of themselves but only to the extent to which they provide a connection with him. ... When stupidity, backwardness or corruption create interference in the lines of communication with the people, energetic measures are taken to restore audibility... In essence, society only trusts the head of state."

In the Middle East, whether it is Israel's desire to preserve its identity at the cost of another people, or Hizballah's grip on its members, motivating them to higher purpose through sacrifice and death, cult behaviour is omnipresent. It is often hidden in the glossy veneer of unquestioned tradition and venerable culture. Culture and cult behaviour are tied together intimately: *Cult u re.*

It is true that no group or country is one static culture, but is a special mix of interrelating smaller cultures. The streetwise homeless in Britain today, for example, have a different culture from a British farmer, accountant or nurse. But simultaneously, all British people share elements that are distinctively different from those of, say, a South American, African or Middle Eastern culture. In other words, each country's mix has a distinct 'flavour.' We all belong to cults by virtue of being part of nations and ethnicities, there is no way around it.

Cults are a powerful, if deeply flawed, mechanism of getting our needs met. As Haidt suggests, we *are* often happy in such groups, enjoying the sense of mission that they provide. Furthermore, putting everyone in line, by following one undisputed path is efficient, which in times of crises, or tribal survival, may be essential.[12] However, the overwhelming trend with cults becomes to *prevail* rather than cooperate. Politics become a test of whose cult is best, or, conversely, a desperate attempt not to be on the losing side.

As someone from the Middle East once told me, "When the wolf lies down with the lamb, we want to make sure we are the wolf."[13] Is it any wonder there is so little cooperation in the Middle East, or in international relations?

We go in and out of cult mode all the time and what counts is how deeply we fall into the cult trap, how unaware we may be of it, and how fixated or flexible we become. Are we at a stage in our evolution where we need better management of this essential trait? The desire for supremacy, an arch trait of the ego, is a telling trait that may need the greatest attention and mastering within the tribe-complex that we are destined to inhabit.

The cult complex cuts to the heart of our political battles and conflicts. The question is do we need to repeat that pattern blindly as we enter an ever more complex future?

THE STARS IN JERUSALEM – CULT CENTRAL

Because religions deal in absolutes, the devaluation of the outsider can be absolute also.

– Arthur Deikman, *Them and Us: Cult Thinking and the Terrorist Threat* [1]

"THE VIA DOLOROSA – The Way of Pain!" Nazmi Al Ju'beh, a Palestinian heritage expert, once warned me, when I told him that I wanted to move to Jerusalem. He turned out to be much more right than I had expected. I had a great passion to live and work in the city, and I can now assure you that the way of passion does lead to the way of pain.

An Israeli psychologist once told me about a Greek who came to Jerusalem. He stayed at the Seven Arches Hotel on the Mount of Olives, came down into the walled Old City to the Via Dolorosa, covered himself with olive oil and set himself on fire in honour of the suffering of his Messiah. He survived but I imagine he was not in good shape. I didn't have this 'Jesus complex' (suffered by individuals who come to the city full of the blind excitement of being at the heart of history).[2] My passion was less dangerous, but it still took me for a volatile ride.

I lived in Jerusalem for three years on 26 Heleni Hamalka Street.[3] I would often look up into the night sky there, black as ink, with a hint of the desert to the east, and enjoy its deep stillness. I had seen a darker sky in Sinai, but that dry, rocky peninsula resembled another planet, an unnatural, skeletal landscape with its granite and basalt mountains, a facsimile of Mars on Earth.[4] Meanwhile, in Jerusalem, one felt at home. The title of Canadian journalist Bronwyn Drainie's book, *My Jerusalem*, encapsulates the problem: *everyone* felt that this was 'home'.

It is true that the city becomes personal like few others. The desire for its possession – political, religious or a combo-deal of the two – is not a far leap from there. We grasp at it as at any desired object, except that it is a 'holy city'.

My favourite Jerusalem was the empty streets of the East side after the Intifadah of 2002. The tourists had run away, and the city was devoid of pilgrims. Its narrow streets, lined by stone walls and empty of cars, permitted an appreciation of its more natural geography. This was certainly not the favourite Jerusalem for the shopkeepers seeking profit, or for youth looking for a modicum of nightlife. "A city should be about girls and hookers, trade and making money, not God. They should put God in the temple!" Shlomo Ben Ami, former Israeli Foreign Minister, complained to me. Like so many secular Israelis, he hated the place, and couldn't wait to get out of there once his workday was done. Indeed, Jerusalem's economy is archaic, based on religious pilgrimage and schools, and an echo of an era long gone.

To many, the city is also a great symbol that is much more important than the people living in it. Across the Islamic world, Jerusalem is the image of the Dome of the Rock, often called Al Aqsa,[5] a symbol of lost glory, and the place from which Muhammad transmigrated to the heavens (the night of Isra' and Mi'raj). In Judaic scripture and exegesis, Jerusalem is the heart of the faith. For Christians across the world, it is the site of the crucifixion of their Lord. Jerusalem is a totem of the human drama, suffering, holy heights and disappointment and, apparently, for the presence of the divine on Earth. For some, Jerusalem is literally, physically, the closest place to God on the planet.

I never appreciated this aspect of the city. I enjoyed friends and good meals, especially in the garden of my Aunt Betty's home (the Aunt Betty who had moved to Jerusalem from Lebanon after marrying the larger than life Palestinian doctor Amin), but it was nature that spoke to me most there. The religious attitudes seemed to me to represent a hidden greed, an abomination despite the scriptural references. It was the very place where people confuse zealotry and emotional excitement with spirituality.

Unlike its moniker as the city of peace, Jerusalem's history is one of intolerance, bloodshed, and the tumbling of walls. From the Crusades to today's oppression, the record is bloodcurdling. In between violent spasms, however, Jerusalem was also often a forgotten backwater. It's only when it occasionally becomes a cause célèbre that anyone pays attention to it. With all that blood, the idea that it is holy seems, on the surface, nonsensical – or maybe the link between blood and the holy, the violent and the sacred, is closer than we think.

Worship in the city was often about stones – the Western Wall, the Rock of Golgotha, the Dome of the Rock, and sometimes it seemed a kind of highly developed paganism in the guise of the so-called monotheistic faiths. Someone explained to me that, on the esplanade of the Al Aqsa Mosque area, the sky was holy as high as it goes (that's quite far). It may well be possible to seek the immanence of God in a place, but appropriating the sky and stones for religio-political purpose seemed rather dangerous.

I resorted to dark humour to manage such absurdities. I

joked that it was Halloween every day there, the Hasidic Jews in their clothing from northern climes, unsuitable for the warmer Mediterranean weather, the Christian nuns and monks mimicking medieval religious garb, and the increasingly conservative Islamic dress, veils and Salafist robes also from another era – all seeking God through a dress code. I often called Jerusalem "cult-central," the city where all forms of cult-mind convened to demonstrate their version of an intense commitment to the divine. More harshly, in the past, the city was described as "a golden basin filled with scorpions."[6]

As we have seen, such attitudes can lead to a readiness to exclude or destroy outsiders. Today, Israel aims to get rid of Arabs and increase the number of Jews in the Holy City. This is an active process, down to the zoning of neighbourhoods and the renaming of city streets. A Palestinian citizen of Jerusalem, whose history there may span back centuries, can lose his Jerusalem residency if the Israeli government finds out that he holds another nationality. At the same time, a Jew from Brooklyn, New York, can immigrate to Israel, and live in the city, without any problem.

Ironically, whoever came to Jerusalem down the years always found it in the possession of another.[7] When the Israelites first arrived the Jebusites were there; when Muslims arrived, Christians were there; when the Crusaders arrived, Muslims were there; and when Zionists arrived, Palestinians were there. However, this did not engender any respect for the other, as many call for; instead, the attachments prevailed over living beings.[8] The *idea* of Jerusalem took precedence over its complex and multifaceted history, as well as its current reality. Today, these fixations and exclusive rights are hallmarks of political prowess, great symbols of our age: whoever is more supreme is greater – that cult and ego thing again.

However, Jerusalem does have an inexplicable magnetism,

and elicits a sense of the ineffable. I felt that often, as did other secular-minded friends. Given the power the city seems to have, maybe Jerusalem would be best as an uninhabited and forested hill. Nature in the city spoke of simpler things, the city's golden stone and violet skies would better be left alone, without our insistent interference.

West of Jerusalem is Ain Karem, a small town that some say St. John the Baptist came from. Around Ain Karem are hills covered by pine, without the pall of human obsession hovering above them. This is what Jerusalem could be, a site with cool air to refresh one's soul and spirit. Without temples, and away from the violent vectors of human greed and compulsion, nature and the creator could be better appreciated, and another kind of religious character would develop.

Was it harsh for me to call this city 'cult-central,' and perceive the religions of the Middle East as cults? Karen Armstrong, an author of many books on comparative religion and the faiths of the Middle East, has made the case that religious wars are fewer and often less violent than other kinds of conflict.[9]

However, while many Westerners drown in apologetics for having colonized the region, I saw levels of religious self-obsession and arrogance in the Middle East that were tough to match. What I remember most about Issam El Orian, a Muslim Brother who loved to cite books, was the moralizing. And, it was the same with Ateret Cohanim, a Jewish settler group that is eating up Jerusalem piece by piece, Hassan Nasrallah, the head of Hizballah, and myriad others. It was their certainties, their unwavering understanding that they were the hands and voice, maybe even the eyes, of God that stuck with me. These sects' sense of conviction had intrigued me but it was an ugly phenomenon up close, and every day we see the results in Mosul, Jerusalem, and Raqqa, an infinite silo of devaluation of others and, from there, a Niagara Falls of violence and conflict.

As Deikman has written, "Because religions deal in absolutes, the devaluation of the outsider can also be absolute." By proposing a privileged link to God, religious authorities encourage the strictest and most powerful form of cult behaviour. They often explain God this way to attract believers who need to feel comforted in a confusing world. Yet, God's representative on Earth, whether son, prophet, text or a chosen people, can also become the ultimate authority figure, the upper pole of the cult-identity axis, going infinitely high. Therefore, religions run the inherent risk of becoming the 'ultimate cults,' and of developing the *ultimate* devaluation of the outsider.

Furthermore, when cultish religious ideas are combined with modern technology and ideology, perfect organisations of destruction can develop. This is what makes terror groups like ISIS, or less extreme but equally ideological groups such as the Iranian Al Quds Force or the Ateret Cohanim, tragically functional: they close off reality, obey, and act with an enthusiastic blindness – while meeting many innate needs.

I hope this goes some distance to explain why religion can lead to violence. When latched on to heated and unprepared minds (and most of us are that), it's built for it.

Jerusalem may be cult-central, but it's also important to remember that the United States is partly founded on a cult: the Puritans, who took enormous risks by moving from Britain to a threatening environment in North America. Their success was again partly due to the advantages of cultdom, a tight group ensuring internal cohesion, especially through fear and respect of the ultimate authority: God.[10]

Karen Armstrong may be statistically correct that religious wars are fewer and less violent than others but, as long as we do not master our cult mind, faith remains fodder for abuse – maybe the best.

PART IV

WE ARE ALL INVOLVED

The fault, dear Brutus, is not in our stars, but in ourselves.

– Shakespeare, *Julius Caesar*, (Act I, scene iii)[1]

THE MANIPULATOR'S ART

It is the demagogue's intuitive knowledge of what men are – as opposed to what they think they are or are told they are – that… makes possible his success.

– Robert Ardrey, *The Territorial Imperative* [1]

All tyranny rests on fraud, on getting someone to accept false assumptions.

– Bergan Evans, *The Natural History of Nonsense* [2]

WE HAVE seen how the components of our ego, the innate basic needs, play out politically, and how our group ego is necessary yet dangerous – and how unaware we are of the ravages of both kinds of self. Our powerful needs impel and compel us blindly; however, most people in the Middle East and elsewhere equate the ego only with their leaders or their enemy. They don't believe or consider that it applies to themselves. Yet, someone who we follow blindly leaves us deeply vulnerable.

I've been a great reader since I was a child and *Moby Dick* is one of the best books I have never fully read. I coursed through it until the whaling ship Pequod was destroyed, and then I was overcome by the book's sweep and detail. Before giving it up, I got a hint of its metaphoric power – the great white fish of our soul inhabiting deepest oceans; our 'fishing expeditions' need to be well prepared or, like the Pequod and its crew, we risk losing all.

Herman Melville wrote another book, far less well known. It is called *The Confidence-Man: His Masquerade* and it involves the Devil as a conman on a Mississippi steamboat, an allegory for how easily people can be manipulated, and it was dedicated to the victims of auto-da-fé. Auto-da-fé was a ritual during the Spanish Inquisition that originally meant "act of faith," and that came to represent burning at the stake. The 'guilty' would wear long pointed caps and a special yellow garment decorated with hellish images of effigies, flames and demons as they were taken to their punishment.

When the Inquisition began in France in the 12th century, it aimed to persecute Beguines, Hussites, Waldensians and Cathars, and other groups we have barely heard of today. They all came under the knife and torch of religious zeal, and were wiped out. The last auto-da-fé took place in Mexico in 1850. Back then, it was the Grand Inquisitor twisting the minds of believers; in our century, it is Abu Bakr El Baghdadi, among others.

Leaders are obviously an important dimension in politics, and people have been manipulated by them since the beginning of time, and this is not a particularly Middle Eastern phenomenon. We have seen earlier how an ISIS recruit had fallen victim to a conman, the silver-tongued Svengali, a used-car salesman who had become a street preacher (both professions that can tempt manipulation).

If critical hidden needs are being hijacked and turned in a destructive direction, someone must be doing the hijacking. But how often do we even realise that we are being manipulated? I suspect that we are mostly unaware, and putty in the hands of those who have an instinct for manipulating our nature.

It all happens so quickly, we watch a leader's speech and are automatically attracted such that we barely have a hold on what is happening to us. Indeed, few of us have ever thought it's even worth examining (even those critical thinkers out there probably fall into the trap once *their* favourite leader espouses truths).

The manipulated have an implicit and unstated pact with the manipulators. "I will follow you if you deliver X, Y and Z for me (whether that is material or emotional benefits)." The pact can be used to build Turkey or Egypt, or any country, or destroy it; it can be used to pursue God constructively or partake in a real-life horror film with the Lord of the Shadows. It all depends on the manipulator's intentions – and, critically, our level of awareness.

People in the Middle East have been taken in by political figures, large or small. Whether admirers of Gamal Abdel Nasser in the 1960s, the followers of Syria's Assads, the worshippers of the Grand Ayatollahs, or more local cults such as that of Rabbi Schneerson in Israel, who was proclaimed *mesiach* (the anointed one) after his death, the readiness to follow quite blindly is omnipresent.

I was lucky enough to meet one such luminary in Lebanon. Appointments with him were top secret and highly staged. I would get into a car in Beirut, switch vehicles, then be driven to the designated meeting spot. The cars were all Mercedes sedans or GM four-wheel drives, and they all moved at high speed, even faster than the usual Indie-500 pace of vehicles in Lebanon.

The man in question was Hassan Nasrallah, the head of Hizballah, and I met him twice in his office in the southern suburbs of Beirut. I was working with the UN and we were asked by headquarters in New York to discuss the kidnapping of two Israeli soldiers by his militant group. It seems that the two had been lured to the fence on the Blue Line to conduct a drug deal and were then set upon by Hizballah fighters and taken prisoner. There was a risk of a violent Israeli reaction to the abduction. As a warning, Israeli fighter jets buzzed Beirut at low altitude, and they were quite loud.

The UN special representative and I met Nasrallah to discuss the possible release of the Israelis, but our talks did not get very far. The UN Secretary General yanked us out after two meetings, and he had his reasons.[3] Nevertheless, the window onto Mr. Nasrallah was telling.

He had a very melodious voice and his charm was both softened and amplified in person, compared with his image on television. Nasrallah conveyed the sense of carrying a larger historical weight, a sense of destiny, if you wish. He conducted talks with a confidence backed by the righteousness of his cause. However, beneath his controlled exterior, he seemed to me to have possibly megalomaniacal traits that knew few bounds.[4]

When I shared my view of him with Lebanese friends I was mostly, and sometimes loudly, dismissed. At the time, in Lebanon, Hassan Nasrallah was untouchable, and my friends defended his pragmatic brilliance as well as the famed discipline of his guerrilla force.

Yet this man and his party were fallible. Hizballah believed the Israeli withdrawal from southern Lebanon was a signal that their enemy was soft, which, in my view, was a fundamental misreading. Such an error of judgment occurred in 2006 when more Israeli soldiers were captured on the border, this time leading to a devastating but unintended war between Hizballah and Israel. That mess was followed by Hizballah's military moves against other Lebanese in 2008, and later, the party's military campaign in support of Syrian President Bashar al-Assad. As a result, many Lebanese became less worshipping of the Hizballah leader than they were in 2000.[5]

Nevertheless, Mr. Nasrallah's ability to command his core following is unshakable. He continues to captivate, and an article in the *New York Times* about Hizballah captures that power: "A sound system played ... anthems – deep male voices booming to a marching band's rhythms. The parents applauded wildly, the mothers ululating ... (the men chanted) You are our leader ... We are your men!"[6] Cult behaviour at its best.

Nasrallah represents but one example of how we can be manipulated by charismatic leaders, and a message that stirs. Voice, language, inner confidence all meld into the shaping of a political dream. During my youth, other leaders' names resonated like divine beings: Jack Kennedy, Charles de Gaulle, Castro, Che Guevara and Martin Luther King, all seemed larger than life. Like the gods in Homer's *Iliad*, they appeared to hover over events, affecting them from above – while we worshipped from below.

Such worship can also take place with less gigantic figures. As David Brooks wrote in a *New York Times* article, "The young British left forms a temporary cult of personality around Jeremy Corbyn. The alienated right forms serial cults around Glenn Beck, Herman Cain, Palin, Trump and Carson."[7] Meanwhile, Chinese "state television showed parliamentarians in tears while Xi Jinping took the oath," reported *Le Monde*.[8] In other words, it's a cross-cultural experience.

Turkey also offers up a case in point. I often went to Istanbul for business meetings, or tourism, and my exposure to young and urbanized Turks led me to believe that they are highly resentful of any efforts to force them to think and behave in certain ways. However, their President, Recep Tayeb Erdogan, is not easily dissuaded. He is the source of love and hate in Turkey.

He and his Justice and Development Party (AKP) were popular because, as small businessman Hassan Senay said, "They connected us in, whereas others counted us out," (in human givens terms: attention, status and belonging).[9] But Mr. Erdogan also believes in changing the life patterns of Turks. He has tried to control alcohol consumption, urged Turks to drink more yogurt, and women to have more babies. Some, like the secular youth, just see a creeping autocracy in all this. The yogurt part is especially concerning.

Ahmet Hakan, a Turkish journalist described the Turkish leader's mentality as follows (with cult characteristics indicated in italics). Mr. Erdogan:

- Believes that his own idea of morality should be adopted by everyone; *(dependency on a leader)*

- Does not even regard it as possible that there may be other moral concepts; *(diminished realism and avoidance of dissent)*

- Divides the lives of his citizens into 'legitimate' and 'illegitimate'; *(devaluation of outsiders)*

- Believes there are parents who want police to monitor the lives of their children; *(avoidance of dissent and group compliance)*

- Has plunged into this matter with all his sincerity ... without considering any strategy, without any doubt that what he is doing is right; *(dependency on the leader)*

- Even worse is that there is not a single person left around Erdogan who has the courage to say, "What you are doing is wrong; you can't do it like this." *(avoidance of dissent and group compliance)*

Haqqan ('truthfully' in Arabic), Hakan is describing exactly how Erdogan drives cult behaviour in the Turkish nation.[10]

This was written quite a few years ago and, since the attempted coup against him of July 2016, his victory in the referendum of 2017, and elections of 2018, these traits may have worsened.

Despite these beliefs, or possibly *because* of them, Mr. Erdogan remains popular in Turkey. He towers from a grand Sultan-like height while some fling mud, and others baklava. However, it's also important to remember that before Mr. Erdogan, there was Mr. Attaturk, whose name means 'Father of the Turks.'[11] To learn who rules over you, find out who you are not allowed to criticise.

All leaders tap into a natural 'operating system' built into us. Their words, speeches and charisma, connect with an innate human resource,[12] which explains why we can fall so easily under their influence. It's not just the conman's masquerade – it's an active mental scam. That innate resource is imagination.[13]

When I was young, I discovered the power of my own. Without knowing it, I would put myself in a trance, completely absorbed in imaginings, ranging from what it would be like to walk on the ceiling, to extra-terrestrials secretly influencing our world. These are all-natural pastimes for a child – I think – but we all still live daily in the thrall of our imaginations. Indeed, as we saw, it was imaginings and longings for the past that took me back to the Middle East in the first place (only to find layers upon layers of political imaginings there).

This kind of imagining is little different from dreaming, except that one occurs in a waking state, the other when asleep. Both are in the theatre of the imagination – the REM (Rapid Eye Movement) state where we are in a trance (dreaming being the trance state supreme).[14] Whether in the dreams of the night, daydreams, or when immersed in intense creativity, that is where we can create worlds and potentially reach great achievement by perceiving beyond immediate reality. Of course, we can go in all directions in that theatre, from the sublime creations of Michelangelo to the ravings of Abu Bakr El Baghdadi.

But, as we can entrance ourselves, so others can entrance us. Hypnosis is any artificial means of inducing the REM trance state, and a trance can be achieved not only via the hypnotist's pendulum but by rhythmic drumming, clapping, repetitive ritual and eliciting strong emotions – "You are our leader ... We are your men." This is where the conmen frolic while we are unaware. Salesmen, preachers, and demagogues hijack and fill our REM state with their vision and ideas, instead of our own - and their egos overcome ours.

How do leaders like Hassan Nasrallah and Turkey's President Erdogan do it so effortlessly? One method is quite subtle. Politicians commonly use 'empty' words – such as 'justice', 'danger', 'freedom', 'change' or 'peace' that can mean different things to different people. Because these are abstractions that do not describe something specific and concrete, our brains are obliged to go on an inner search to find out what they mean *to us individually*: we enter our imaginations to do that. What does 'peace' mean? I have to imagine it. For one person it might be getting their home back; for another, a deal with Assad; for yet another, revenge on the enemy. The possibilities are many.

Once we are mentally consumed in trying to figure out what

such empty words mean to us personally, we are in that trance state, no longer questioning and thus vulnerable to a politician who can manipulate us into following his script. Entranced, we are deeply available to whatever the ladies and gentlemen are pouring into our mental cup.

To see this in action, we only have to watch former American president, Donald Trump, who was attacked regularly for his lies and excesses, and yet has entranced millions into voting for him. However, it is worthwhile to pay attention to more subtle acts of persuasion. Former President Obama's slogans about change were also equivocal and confusing to the mind. The words 'great' and 'change' raise our emotions, but mean different things to everyone who hears them; no two people's wants are exactly the same. Although his actions were less dramatic and destructive than Trump's, Obama used the same powerful mechanism of what is effectively deceit (even if we have accepted it as 'normal' since time immemorial).

There is an even darker aspect to all this. Once our attention is locked in the REM state, basically hypnotized, we are highly focused on imagining, ignore all our surroundings, and no longer see larger contexts – that fixated mind in action, once again. Without that wider view, we can become less empathetic: 'them and us' thinking is induced, and we are ready to make enemies. Trump's early targeting of Muslim and Hispanic populations is testament to this dark art.

Even more likeable figures such as Bernie Sanders, the great left hope, used the manipulator's art and the binary, them and us effect. He often positions the average citizen against the big banks creating black and white scenarios of good and bad guys, and then heightens emotions to get the point across by creating fear, anger and resentment.

Leaders in democracies are not tyrants per se, but that does not mean that we are truly politically free in their hands either.

There is also a cruder and literally louder method to accomplish the mission. I saw it play out frequently in the Middle East on television, when leaders made their speeches, and after Friday prayers, when the local sheikh whipped up the believers through an intense and fiery sermon. Sometimes, it was simply at a dinner, when a loudmouth stunned other guests into submission by a high-volume attack on an enemy. All that high emotion had a purpose: move the crowd in your direction. The loud voice and aggression make the listener submissive, without him or her realising it.

"He's always shouting!" said a Turkish shopkeeper about Erdogan's very frequent speeches.[15] In this competition for our attention, it is a race to the bottom; the more garish and crude win out over the subtle and sophisticated. Emotions trump facts (there's a pun in there somewhere).[16] Indeed, "In an age when politics are so well scripted and sanitized ... it is refreshing when you have anger and even hatred which reflects [the people's] own feelings," said Asli Aydintasbas, a former journalist and senior fellow at the European Council on Foreign Relations, about Turkish president Erdogan's style of speechmaking.[17]

Since time immemorial, politicians have used what are effectively conmen's tricks to gain followers. It is such a common part of our political life that we don't really question it, but it sadly comes at a cost: citizens stop thinking and become putty in their hands.

Humans fall for the art of the con man, with often fatal consequences because we are unaware of the workings of our minds. Some see through it, like Susan Aylward, who said: "The notion that strong individuals can bend the world to their will is compelling. It is also deeply flawed. That's what we're taught to believe from an early age ... We're taught that one man should be able to fix everything. Abe Lincoln, George Washington, Ronald

Reagan – history's told as though it were all down to them. The world is way too complex for that."[18]

Donald Trump, Hassan Nasrallah, Vladimir Putin, Recep Tayyip Erdogan and many others occupy our mental space much as others occupy territory. To de-occupy, step one is not street protests – it is to become aware of how we fall for the game of hypnosis in our politics. The natural human desire to be manipulated can only be cured by education about the way our minds work (and a desire to grow up and do our own thinking, God forbid).

A few years ago, I saw on the internet the following words attributed to a great leader: "Beware the leader who bangs the drums of war in order to whip the citizenry into a patriotic fervour, for patriotism is indeed a double-edged sword. It both emboldens the blood, just as it *narrows the mind*. And when the drums of war have reached a fervour pitch and the blood boils with hate and the *mind has closed* the leader will have no need in ceasing the rights of the citizenry. Rather, the citizenry, infused with fear and blinded by patriotism, will offer up all of their rights unto the leader and gladly so. How do I know? This is what I have done." It was supposedly Julius Caesar who is quoted here, although there is no actual evidence that he said this. The words are nevertheless a perfect depiction of what happens to our minds through leaders' manipulations.

As Turkish opposition leader Meral Aksener said about President Erdogan, "Friend, please keep silent for a moment; spare a little bit of time for your family; sit at home. You don't have to talk about every issue. You don't have to point out your finger everywhere... Take a breath, so we can take breath too, so Turkey can." [19]

TRUMP'S WORLD – OUR WORLD: THE PROBLEM IS NOT JUST OUR LEADERS

The foundation of tyranny in the world was trifling at first.
Everyone added to it until it attained its present magnitude.

– Saadi Shirazi, in *The Way of the Sufi* [1]

WHEN THE NERVE gas poisoning of a Russian dissenter Sergei Skripal and his daughter Yulia took place in Salisbury, in the UK, apparently authorised by the Kremlin, the Russian population saw a complete disconnect between themselves and their leaders. They do not believe they are connected with, or are responsible for, what their rulers do, and I have seen identical attitudes in the Arab world.

As a Russian psychologist says of his country, "the rabble never consider themselves guilty; it always views itself as the victim. It sincerely thinks that others must sympathize and understand them" without any sense that they must sympathize (with) and understand others. Their view is that [Russian's] security organs are "your [the West's] problem. We simply live here."[2]

Most people don't wish to examine themselves, natural laziness or a presumption that one is already right, ensure that. Indeed, they do their utmost to avoid any responsibility by choosing a leader who will take care of things for them. Manipulative and ill-willed leaders then turn around and foist all the risk and downside on those very citizens, and so the world turns.

I sit in a typical living room in the Middle East. The discussion rapidly turns to who controls the world, and what devious plot is being hatched against the locals. One case that really opened my eyes was the story that some believed that the Malaysia Airlines Flight 370 jet, which went missing in 2014, had been taken by the CIA to the military island base of Diego Garcia in the Indian Ocean in order to capture an important foreign military officer. Maybe his name was Jason Bourne.

Conspiracy theories abound across the world. They are neat stories to explain complicated events, or even mere accidents. NATO conspires with the Queen of England to murder Princess Diana. In Lebanon, some cows and wild pigs that drift across the Blue Line, the border between Israel and Lebanon, likely looking for some tasty grass, are thought to be instruments of Israeli espionage. An Algerian diplomat insisted to me that Egypt's former president Hosni Mubarak, the Saudi royalty and many other Arab rulers were all Jews destroying the Arab world. She meant literally that they were Jews – the exception was Saddam Hussein, whom she admired.

But the story that topped it all appeared when I left Egypt after my posting in 1996: I read that the Zionists had spread an aphrodisiac-laced chewing gum across the country to corrupt the morality of Egyptian youth, especially girls. The plot was even raised by a parliamentarian who accused Israel of "a huge scheme to ravage the young population of Egypt."[3]

Not all notions of conspiracy are that dramatic. One person in the Middle East once told me that the Americans were behind the radical Islamists in Syria, while, a few days later, another highly educated individual insisted that the US was conspiring to keep Assad, the Islamists' very enemy, in place. Maybe the Americans were using the Algerian diplomat's favourite Jewish-Arab leaders to do so.

Another Algerian friend was recently posted to Cairo for a UN job. After several months there, she told me that she was shocked by the degree of high emotion, opinion and conspiratorial thinking she had experienced – and she's a fellow Arab. "It is quite easy to understand the terrible current political situation once you deal with people in the streets on a daily basis," she said. "It is surprising how much extremism there is in everything. And by this, I don't only mean religious extremism. Even so-called intellectual people explain the situation using conspiracy and extreme opinion as an argument."

It seems we have in our brains a Hyperactive Agency Detector Device (HADD, a term coined by American cognitive scientist Justin Barrett), which might go part way towards explaining all this. We are hyperactive at seeing 'agency' around us; we impute intentional motives to objects or people, trees, clouds, our neighbours – it doesn't matter what or who. We do this because it paid off long ago to err on the side of caution. Better to think that rustle in the bushes is a tiger, and turn out to be wrong.

However, the HADD puts us on high alert, which lends itself to cut outs of the world, and may be needed in an emergency. But in the Middle East, people are on high alert <u>all the time</u> – it is the zone of SHADD, the Super Hyperactive Agency Detector Device.[4] This is partly why conspiracies fly so easily, why paranoia is rampant, and why there is also a kind of pessimism and endless worrying in the air. The Middle East's long history has led the people there to conclude that the tiger is indeed just around the corner...

Less dramatic than conspiracy, but potentially just as damaging, is political *opinion*: an unquestioned set of personal assumptions about the world and how it works that could well be wrong. When I was dealing with issues on the Blue Line between Lebanon and Israel, Lebanese who had little to do with politics would corner me at a cocktail party and ask, "What is going on with the Shebaa Farms issue," referring to a small strip of land disputed between Israel, Lebanon and Syria. Before I could even get the canape out of my mouth to respond, the interlocutor would deliver his opinion with vehemence. He was clearly only asking in order to inform me of the reality. Almost no one in Lebanon or anywhere else knows much about this arcane issue, my presence just provided an opportunity for them to demonstrate their unabashed ignorance – while I kept eyeing the canapes. (I have done considerable research on the matter, and still fail to understand the question of sovereignty of the Shebaa Farms.)

Shark Wilson is the name of a reggae band, but it's also shorthand for what happened to President Woodrow Wilson in 1916. There was a deadly rash of shark attacks on the Jersey shore during that year and, as a result, Wilson lost his home state in the presidential election. Unless you're a conspiratorialist or a fan of magic mushrooms, neither Mr. Wilson nor his opponent could be held responsible for the shark attacks; however, as a result, the voters, especially the beachfront owners who lost tourism revenue, were no longer in any mood to re-elect the incumbent President.

According to political scientists Christopher Achens and Larry Bartels "Voters don't have anything like coherent preferences. Most people pay little attention to politics; when they vote, if they vote at all, they do so irrationally and for contradictory reasons."[5] The greater point about all of the above – conspiracy or opinion – is that most people develop political ideas without any thought about their validity, and then they marry them. Sadly, "the typical citizen drops down to a lower level of mental performance as soon as he enters the political field."[6] If you combine that with the readiness of some leaders to manipulate as we had seen above, then the room for massive error and tragedy is rather significant.

David Dunning from Cornell University warns that the internet is helping propagate such ignorance. It serves as an amplification device, spinning opinions into hyperbolic space. It's a place where everyone has a chance to be a self-made expert. This also makes people prey to powerful interests wishing to deliberately spread certain views. More information can even *polarize* people's attitudes.[7]

Dunning argues that incompetent people are inherently unable to judge the competence of others, or the quality of others' ideas: "The democratic process relies on the assumption that citizens (the majority of them, at least) can recognize the best political candidate, or best policy idea, when they see it [but] this may simply not be the case. No amount of information or facts about political candidates can override the inherent inability of many voters to accurately evaluate [expertise]."[8]

No matter where one sits on the spectrum between fantastical conspiracy and political opinion, the result of all this is the dumbing down of democracy. Watching electoral coverage across the world, anywhere, can only lead us to conclude that the political conversation has slipped rather considerably. The *Princeton Review* found that the US presidential Lincoln–Douglas debates of 1858 were engaged at roughly a high-school senior level. A century later, the presidential debate of 1960 was a notch below that, at a 10th grade level. By the year 2000, the two contenders were speaking like sixth graders. And in the 2016 debates – 'Crooked Hillary' against 'Don the Con' – we were lucky to get beyond pre-school potty talk."[9]

Politics is perceived as everybody's business, and thus we have the right to have an opinion about it, right or wrong (mostly wrong). Yet, whether we recognize it as such or not, this is really another, more subtle form of political ego: whatever I think is valid, because it's mine.

The Persian poet Saadi's words at the beginning of this section are insightful: the problems in politics are not just with the elites, they are an accumulation from top to bottom in an all-consuming celebration of ignorance. Some vote-in strange leaders as answers to their problems, others join dangerous groups. We all contribute to the great arc of descent; we are all involved. An atmosphere of anxiety due to unmet needs can ensure poor choices.

In America, no fewer than 62,979,636 people voted for Donald Trump in 2016. That's more than the population of 21 countries in the world, larger than the populations of Italy or South Africa, and that number grew in 2020 by almost 12 million to 74,222,958.

Here is a journalist's report about some of the supporters of Donald Trump before he was elected in 2016: "The Trump supporters I spoke with were friendly, generous with their time, flattered to be asked their opinion, willing to give it, even when they knew I was a liberal writer likely to throw them under the bus. They loved their country, seemed genuinely panicked at its perceived demise, felt urgently that we were, right now, in the process of losing something precious.

"They were, generally, in favour of order... They leaned

toward scepticism... They were anti-regulation, pro small business, pro Second Amendment, suspicious of people on welfare, sensitive (in a 'don't tread on me' way) about any infringement whatsoever on their freedom.

"The average Trump supporter is not the rally pugilist, the white supremacist, the bitter conspiracy theorist, though these exist and are drawn to Trump... and, at times, the first flowerings of these tendencies were present among some of the rank-and-file supporters I met."[10]

The key phrases to me here are "losing something precious" and "don't tread on me." These are indicators of strong emotion at play that, when combined with ignorance, can lead to poor political choices. Although the Trump voters may have valid reasons for their dissatisfaction, their choice for a fix possibly created unimagined new problems for their country.

When the citizens' needs are unmet, this leaves them in anxiety and prone to poor decisions. Strong emotions can narrow down our focus of attention, necessarily so in order that we can pay proper attention in an emergency, but in doing so they effectively render us less intelligent. If the Middle East can be defined by anything it is high emotion, and you can extract the corollary from there. Under stress and high emotion resulting from unmet needs, or social conditioning by our group and culture, we not only don't make the best decisions; *we may simply stop thinking at all.*

The fault is not just with our leaders, we are all at play, and when it comes to politics, a solid understanding of our own behaviour is close to zero. Everyone adds to the problem until it attains its present magnitude.

NEEDS MET BADLY:
THE ROAD TO DESTRUCTION

ALTHOUGH the average citizen contributes to the problem, it is most often he or she that suffers disproportionately. My colleague, Ivan Tyrrell, and I once gave a presentation to a meeting in Beirut to introduce analysts, officials and journalists to a better understanding of the psychological root causes of violent extremism: we suggested the Human Givens approach as a basis for thinking about a way forward.

Many others of those present talked about regional politics instead – Iran behind Hizballah, Saudi behind Daesh – matters that are certainly important and interesting to discuss. The meeting however diverged, two ships passing in the night, with one set of participants trying to understand the basic motivations of terrorists, the other fixed on the macro-ideological.

After that conference I returned home by taxi, and the driver and I started talking. He informed me that Lebanese politicians "do everything except care about the human being. Everything is done but what we need. We are all in a state of total anxiety and we can't function." He was desperate for some improvement in traffic and electricity, and some signal that his government cared about him, his children, and his future.

This was exactly what Ivan and I had been telling the elites the day before. If citizens' basic needs are not met, anxiety and high emotion and all sorts of odd behaviour will set in, including 'gilets jaunes' and, in extremis, violent extremism. This is not to say that this poor taxi driver would become an extremist, but that the political environment was ripe for violent and chaotic developments.[1] What has happened in Lebanon since is a testament to this truth. It is a country bereft of consideration for basic needs, material and emotional.

However, the drive to have emotional needs meet is so strong that we will usually try to meet them somehow, even if it's destructive for ourselves and others to do so. *How* we meet these needs matters enormously.

Corruption & Mafia States

I know an immigrant to Canada who was unprepared culturally and educationally for his new country. He tried his hand at regular work, started a corner shop and worked in sales, but he was somehow temperamentally not suited for this kind of basic effort. It was possibly the way he had been raised. He hadn't bothered to learn a new craft, with all the pain and discipline required; he grabbed whatever opportunity made sense to him as a means to get his needs met, no matter the consequences. He ultimately ended up finding his way to mafia-like activities with some cultural brethren – and that's a euphemism.

When people can't have their needs met in healthy ways, they will do so in unhealthy ways – in the above person's case, the need for belonging, status, and meaning (and his material needs) were met in the easiest way possible. He has had many Cadillacs.

Today, 'mafia states' are developing across the world, elites running countries through threat and for profit, just like the Cosa Nostra does but with a little patriotism on top, and many are content with this offering.

The mafia-state often first takes over the critical state security systems. The poorly paid police have much to gain because the mafia-state provides them with state legitimacy, as well as more cash gained through the nefarious activities. Through threat and coercion, they then drain states of their public goods while still offering some degree of material gain for the citizen.

Importantly, they often dose the process with some binding nationalism, and a spirit of group cohesion that can be used to increase the level of threat to anyone against the system. Excommunication, prison and torture are the mechanisms of enforcement. "The state is... privatized as a family business. The power of obedience is based on a combination of loyalty, repression and political economics," said French social scientist Emmanuel Todd. [2]

For many, there isn't much choice anyway; once these gangs hijack the system, you are hostage to their demands. If you don't work with them, you will be poor; if you criticize them you may end up in jail, or dead. Mafia-like operations are not much different from extremist groups in that they provide for many basic needs, if at a heavy price for the individual and the society around them.[3]

For many citizens, the sense of security, economic opportunity and national pride that mafia states engender are enough. Benefits of more open societies, such as freedoms and individual rights, are temporarily put aside for this package.

As a result, according to democracy expert Larry Diamond, "Around 2006, the expansion of freedom and democracy in the world came to a prolonged halt. Since 2006, there has been no net expansion in the number of electoral democracies, which has oscillated between 114 and 119 (about 60 percent of the world's states) ... Since 2006 the average level of freedom in the world has also deteriorated slightly.

"Since 2000 [there have been] 25 breakdowns of democracy

in the world – not only through blatant military or executive coups, but also through subtle and incremental degradations of democratic rights and procedure... Some of these breakdowns occurred in quite low-quality democracies; yet in each case, a system of reasonably free and fair multiparty electoral competition was either displaced or degraded to a point well below the minimal standards of democracy."

Thomas Friedman adds, "Vladimir Putin's Russia and Erdogan's Turkey are the poster children for this trend, along with Venezuela, Thailand, Botswana, Bangladesh and Kenya. In Turkey ... the AKP has steadily extended partisan control over the judiciary and the bureaucracy, arresting journalists and intimidating dissenters in the press and academia, threatening businesses with retaliation if they fund opposition parties, and using arrests and prosecutions in cases connected to alleged coup plots to jail and remove from public life an implausibly large number of accused plotters. This has coincided with a stunning and increasingly audacious concentration of personal power by... Erdogan. Rule of law in Turkey is being seriously eroded."[4][5]

Importantly, the citizen is fully involved and complicit. If Erdogan can deliver 6.5 percent growth since 2010, many Turks are quite happy to support him, whatever system he puts forward. A less corrupt life, and an honest living, become increasingly out of fashion; the new role models are gangsters with black Mercedes – or Cadillacs. The bottom line is that if these mafia models deliver, especially materially combined with a dose of Gumilevian patriotism, many will say 'why not?'

But, this can be a short-term outlook. A focus only on profits and nationalistic highs can have consequences. The average citizen, including my taxi driver friend, can also be out of luck. Lake Mariout will turn pink with pollution, there will be no water available in Sanaa, Yemen and, indeed, the taxi driver's children will suffer more than he does today because the system is gamed for the gain of a few, while all else, such as infrastructure and the environment, are ignored. Possibly, most importantly, the natural human need for some autonomy and freedom is squelched. But, this seems like a detail if you are after fast money.

In a book called *Thieves of State*, Sarah Chayes also shows how corruption can breed resentment among some citizens, and even ultimately violent extremism as a way to right unfairness. Some join the dollar merry-go-round, but others fume. Extremists or other ideological manipulators urge the angry citizen to join them to fix things together. Chayes believes that the overthrow of Mubarak was directly linked to his incompetent and corrupt economic policies. Egyptians saw the regime "as the direct product of corrupt practices perpetrated by an upstart clique of crony capitalists who had captured key levers of the Egyptian state and were using them to advance their private agenda."[6]

She also makes the powerful point that, in many countries, ranging from Afghanistan to Nigeria to Uzbekistan, it is such social justice that people are looking for, not just ideals of democracy and human rights. Social justice means that our status is not lower than that of others, and that our groups' cohesion is not being corroded by cheaters.[7] Corruption destroys trust, the essential ingredient for any smooth running of human relations. Chayes demonstrates that many of the Taliban were primarily motivated by a perception that their government was irrevocably corrupt, and they saw violent action as a necessary means to correct this immoral state of affairs.

The price of having a mafia-state can be high. On August 4, 2020, a very large explosion took place in the port of Beirut, decimating a section of the city and causing hundreds of deaths and wounding thousands. Although the exact sequence of events that caused the explosion will likely never be known, we can link the event to the rise of the mafia-state in Lebanon. Most likely, a nefarious alliance between the Hizballah militia, which has stores of munitions and explosives throughout the country and which used Beirut's port as an entry point for its needs as well as those of the Assad government (its ally in the Syrian war), and corrupt politicians and their underlings meant that explosive materials were stored in this dangerous location, and were set off by accident or malice. Needs get met but at high costs and inefficiencies, and often with violent results.

The Problem with Prosperity

Significant problems do not just occur in mafia-states. In an entertaining and insightful book called *The Price of Prosperity: Why Rich Nations Fail and How to Renew Them,* American economist Todd G. Buchholz points to other key causes of the disintegration of societies. Countries fall apart, he says, because of increased wealth and its consequences: "Nations are just as likely to unravel after periods of prosperity as during periods of depression… Rising incomes sparked more ethnic conflict than stagnant incomes did in prior eras."[8] According to Buchholz, citizens become less concerned with the state and public affairs when they become more materially self-sufficient. They also then have fewer children, and changes in demographics take place as foreign labour pours in to do the jobs that the now wealthier citizens reject.

Wealth breeds a prized but dangerous individualism that results in a loss of national purpose, and, as a result, the social fabric decays. This is not a new theory and many observant people throughout history have pointed out the negative effects of wealth and its partner, corruption, that comes along for the ride. Money makes the world go round, but too much makes nations disintegrate – you just can't win.

Despite this reality, the main economic objective of most countries remains increased income and wealth creation – the very cause of their undoing. This is because *the idea* of ever greater wealth provides us with a fantasy of happiness: he who dies with the most toys wins. Yet, ironically, it all adds up to a gnawing hunger as another part of our selves remains dissatisfied with material gain, no matter how great. Greed, or the unlimited pursuit of needs, is as dangerous as lack, and we would all do well to heed Buchholz's warning about the price of prosperity.

As long as we are unaware of our vital emotional needs, the political animal will predate and move in any direction available to be satisfied in the short term, from criminality to mounds of material splendour.

LIKE FATHER, LIKE SON

*If the "ordinary folk" would make themselves worthwhile,
then they would be able to guide affairs, not just form
the cannon-fodder.*

– Idries Shah [1]

IN JANUARY 2011, the Tunisian revolution kicked off. At the time, I happened to be at a meeting in Brussels where two former Egyptian diplomats were present. During my time as a Canadian diplomat I lived for three years in Egypt – a country whose civilization seemed much older than that of the rest of the region. It was once known by another name, Kemet, the ancient Egyptian word for 'black,' after its rich soil, the accumulation of the silt deposits of the Nile winding their way to sea.

I lived in Kemet in the 1990s and lost half my hair because of the stresses of Cairene life, pollution, noise, traffic and all. Nevertheless, I also learned to appreciate the country and to see it as a great organism that bound its people since ancient times through its life-giving river. As Lebanon's geography divided, the Nile united. Egypt was a nation-state before all others, and Egyptian identity was far less up for question than in the querulous Levant. Egyptians were not great entrepreneurs like the

Lebanese or Syrians, but their ready acceptance of their compatriots was seamless – or so it used to be.

The two highly talented Egyptian diplomats assured the gathered group in Brussels that no version of the Tunisian revolt would happen in their country. Egypt was exceptional; it was different.[2]

A few days later, in Madrid, I watched on television as the Egyptian revolution broke out. Like many others, I was awed by the rapid, peaceful, mass overthrow of tyranny. I itched to be there, in what seemed to be almost a fantasy: the successful rise of Arab youth to depose oppressive authority. It was even more uplifting because it wasn't even ideological – friends in the square attesting to an almost ineffable occasion. I was initially more optimistic about these events than the Oslo Accords because they were spontaneous and socially rooted, rather than a cook-up by elites.

In January 2012, I made a point of going to Tahrir Square to attend the first anniversary of the Egyptian revolution. This time, I watched the events 'live' from the apartment of a friend of a friend, who had kindly invited me there, along with others. His home sits right above Tahrir, filled with sketches of cats and nude women, dust-covered antique furniture, and mashrabiah (an element of traditional Arabic architecture) melding into one – all very Cairene, especially the dust.

From his balcony, we could see the mass convocation below, stretching from the Egyptian Museum to the government building known as the Mugamaa, to the Nile, creating that strange buzz that large numbers of humanity in one place produce.[3] The spirit of 2011 was there again, amidst the roasted sweet potato vendors, the funky Salafists, and the marchers for women's rights. The political parties were shouting their ideologies left and right through megaphones, and there was a carnival atmosphere, a sense of open space and an Arab agora. It all spelled possibility and there was little care for the consequences, at least for the time being.

As I looked down at Tahrir, I had a good discussion with a Salafist about the future of Egypt. He assured me that he considered leftists and Copts his brethren, but he was more doubtful about the Muslim Brothers. I also spoke with an Italian Marxist who believed the communist dialectic was unfolding right before his eyes. He had been on a beach in Bari, or wherever he came from, when he had a vision that he must come to Cairo and witness the great unfolding take place, and there he was. I descended into the crowd with Mr. Marx Italia. He waded through the masses, shaking hands with whomever he could grab. It was as if he was running for office, and many greeted him with great affection – and no one cared.

Of course, this sense of 'no one cares' cannot carry a country forward. The very next day, there was a football riot in the city of Port Said that resulted in many deaths. New demonstrations in Cairo ensued, this time aimed at the notorious Ministry of Interior, which was blamed for the casualties at the football stadium. I witnessed those events as well, but they were more ominous than Tahrir. 'Ultras,' football fanatics who specialized in aggressive demonstrations, moved towards the walled-off streets around the Ministry to confront the security troops. I was far from the battle lines, where some were losing eyes or choking on teargas, but I could still see that this was no out-of-control mob scene. Even when attacked or provoked, the protest groups remained restrained and organized.

It was Egyptian youth that led the protests. The pursuit of excitement and action had lured them away from otherwise dull lives. I was told that this was especially the case for the kids of Boulaq, a poor neighbourhood just beside Tahrir.[4] They were frustrated and desperate for change, many of them with little to lose, and they simply spilled over into the action taking place around the corner.

The Arab revolutions happened without any organizing framework to hold the competing dynamics together – and so they fell apart. Having lived under tyranny for decades, few had the disciplined yet independent mind that would enable them to be the freethinking citizens that the revolutions demanded. Crucial political steps, such as the development of a new constitution, had to be invented on the spot. Only Tunisia has since demonstrated some signs of success, and it may be the proverbial exception that proves the rule.

Reality turned out to be more complicated than that positive moment in Tahrir and turmoil soon followed in Egypt. The more organized, motivated and well-funded groups, usually ideological and often Islamist, grabbed the liberated political space. In Syria, Yemen and Libya, the competition between political forces and self-interest led to the disintegration of nations. The spirit of the revolution that I had experienced in Tahrir – free, emancipated humans for a day – would not only be ineffable; it would be evanescent. The hopeful events of Tahrir and Tunis were transformed into the destruction of Aleppo and Sanaa. Having erased some of the stale torpor of the last 20 years and indulged in a sharp and exciting spike of hope, the Arab world then crashed into the abyss. Rollercoaster ride over.

It is now estimated that the cost of the Arab revolutions is around $600 billion, money that could have been spent on more durable societal and political change if a more responsible government and body politic existed.[5] My heart sank. My darker convictions about the region had been confirmed: it was a false dawn.

Tahrir ironically means liberation in Arabic, but the Middle East and its people were far from free, and it was not just a question of leaders having strayed from responsibility. The exit from the madhouse would need more knowledge and time.

I visited Egypt one year later, in 2013. This was not the Egypt that I knew and had felt affection for. The society was confused about its direction and unhappy about its current (elected) masters, the Muslim Brothers. It was bereft of tourists, and all I heard were complaints about the governing party. There was a seething hatred against them, worse than that against 'the tyrant,' former President Mubarak.

On June 30, 2013, Egyptians demonstrated in the hundreds of thousands to get rid of the Muslim Brotherhood government. The citizens were once again in Tahrir, happy that the army, part of the very establishment that they had previously revolted against, was leading the overthrow. Why did Egyptians, including liberals, run back into the lap of the army, a group fundamentally against their revolutionary aims?

"Most people think of fear as running away from something. But there is another side to it. We run TO someone (or something), usually a person," says Alexandra Stein, an expert on attachments to totalitarian systems.[6] When the economy tanked, and order and security drifted out of reach, the search for a new authority figure began. Egyptians sought someone to come and take care of their problems – and them. And, in this case, his name was General Sisi, who was shortly after sworn in as Egypt's sixth president.

Egyptians call their country *Umm ed-Dunya* or 'Mother of the World.' If I asked them who, then, was 'father of the world', they would look at me with surprise. Then, after a short pause, some would answer, "America is *Abu ed-Dunya*, father of the world."

The father figure in the Arab world is the one who 'knows best,' at home, at work, in government, and in religion. Respect for that authority is a pillar of Arab culture, and that extends to the top father in the country: Mr. Ruler. Internationally, 'Amreeka,' with all its military and economic might, is perhaps not surprisingly, perceived as father of the world. Israel, America's godchild, is seen as an extension of that father's authoritarian oppression.

The problem is father figures and authorities also breed their own enemy in the shape of rebels. Radical and fanatic opposition to them evolves naturally and 'father killers' emerge, seeking revenge for being oppressed, striking at the barriers in their way. While in Libya, after Ghaddafi, the result was mayhem as a thousand sons of a thousand towns fought it out for control, in Syria the authority–tyrant was powerful enough, with sufficient support from inside and out, to destroy his country in the fight against the rebels.

A sad and difficult truth results: many of these rebels spring from the same political culture as the tyrants they purport to hate. They are authoritarianism-and-tyranny version 2 and want to establish *themselves* as the new and undisputed masters of the universe. Their goal is to get rid of the old oppressor so that <u>they</u> can wield power instead; they do not necessarily represent a new, more liberal order. Like father, like son - or maybe worse.

Daesh, Maesh, Ansar this, Jibhat that, all those radical groups are not seeking freedom of mind; they instead strive to be the new (and purer) authority, with all the benefits that accrue. For it is their turn to be top dog.

It was partly the culture, the very habits of nations, and poor adaptations to circumstances, that meant that one set of tyrants would only be replaced by another. It became clear to me that changing the structures of government, or demanding rights was not enough. The problem was among both citizens and leaders. Few are immune to the blindness and power of the ego. The real battle for the decent demonstrators lies in changing the habits that created the problem in the first place, which in turn requires a better understanding of our nature.

If we harken back to the quote at the beginning of this section, "If the "ordinary folk" would make themselves worthwhile, then they would be able to guide affairs, not just form the cannon-fodder." Idries Shah, the scholar and writer, continues to say, "but this is not easy. It is easier to work on the primitive level, to arrange a mass rally and demonstrate than to improve oneself."[7]

The reality may be that street protests are more reflective of the disease than the cure. The system may need a shock, but sustained and sustainable reform is the real game.

As Maya Baydoun, a Lebanese journalist, said: "The day that Lebanese youth start ridding themselves of worshipping their leaders and warlords, and start electing representatives based on merit not religion, then and only then will Lebanon become a developed country. In the meantime, what's going on is shallow protest and definitely not a revolution."

We are all involved, in commission and omission. The shift ahead is more significant than a change in leaders or political structures. We need not look to the stars for answers, the shift is ironically closer to home, in ourselves, tapping into our very natures to navigate the currents and eddies that lie ahead.

MASTERING THE POLITICAL EGO

The summary of the advice of all prophets is this:
Find yourself a mirror.

– Shams of Tabriz [1]

THE BOTTOM LINE:
ANA WA BAS

We are the people who do not compromise.
For us, it is supremacy over others or death.[1]

ONE DAY, walking in East Jerusalem on a pleasant spring day, I saw some graffiti scribbled on a wall. It was the ugliest happy face that I have ever seen, with a smile, a squint and fangs, and below it was written in Arabic, "*ana wa bas*": "me and only me."

In that face, I saw the Middle East of today, its politics and sometimes its culture, "I" before anyone else – whether that "I" is defined as self, family, tribe, party, religion or nation. That 'ana' is that part of us focused solely on ourselves, our own survival or gain, rather than on something larger. Blindness, fantasy, opinion and the desire for supremacy are its manifestations. As we have seen, many of our basic needs, whether the search for attention, status, or pride in our group, are aspects of the ego. There is little wrong with them, they are necessary for our survival, unless greed or a desire for supremacy inform them.

An out of control ego can become automatic and cause or lead to associative forms of consciousness that enslave us to a form of sleep – even if it feels like reality. There, destructive cut outs of the world abet a vast cacophony of manipulation and destruction. At its worst, it taps into deeper, archetypal forms of darkness, and then, well, we're really in a bit of trouble.

An old Sufi term for the ego is the Commanding Self.[2] It is useful because the ego not only commands us to do its bidding, it also aims to control others in an endless game of one-upmanship: "supremacy over others or death." Sufis say the Commanding Self has to be tamed before we can become fully human – thus the title of this book.

In the Middle East, the Commanding Self is very much alive. Its political manifestations include the triumph of tyrants, self-perpetuating conflicts, and demands for infinite retribution for past injustice (yes, even that can be egoistical if it denies today's realities). Powerful groups such as Hizballah (the Party of God), ideas of a superior Jewish destiny in the region, as well as every single crazy driver on the Lebanese highways, reflect its power and drive for supremacy. It is every attempt to make one's own group prevail, to get away with things whenever possible, and to lie one's way to short-term advantage (*shatahra* in Arabic, which also means 'cleverness').

This translates into daily dishonesty and distrust. Meetings are held and agreements come to, but afterwards each participant feels the right to ignore consensus through a private veto, because 'I' am the most important. The self-importance and puffed-up pride deny the validity of others, even one's own deeper (and more satisfying) principles, in favour of the immediate. And the world becomes either/or, with me or against me; the greys disappear, and the unit trumps the whole. Everyone takes advantage before being taken advantage of, and the fangs of the Commanding Self become even more finely honed indeed.

Over a lifetime, such habits can morph into endless greed

and grandiose appetites. The desire to possess Jerusalem, the destruction of Aleppo, Beirut's pollution, the megalomaniacal speeches of Hassan Nasrallah, the mother using emotional blackmail to keep her children near her, the exaggerated pride of the Arab male, the power of conspiracy and opinion – all are the Commanding Self showing its might. From parent to child, from the mosque to television, the tyranny of authority and the habit of grasping and the 'command' is passed on in the broken culture of the region, a kind of self-perpetuating mark of Cain. This force spreads its wings wide and becomes a world with 'Ana wa bas' as its theme song.

Is there really more to the problems of Israel and Palestine, the destruction of Syria or the collapse into corruption and greed of the Arab world than 'ana wa bas'?

It is what is behind the desire to cut a tomb in half, own a temple, or deny another people's existence. "We are the people who do not compromise."

The Commanding Self works through the mortal twins of negative and positive expectation, pleasure and pain, hope and fear – no greys, only Them and Us. Interestingly, it links enemies together in hidden ways. Whether the USA and Russia, Assad and ISIS, or the darker sides of both Israelis and Palestinians, they really are on the same side: *that which is only for itself.* Consciously or not, they concoct a joint cacophony, one that many of us then join in unwittingly.

An example of how this takes place is when Donald Trump (a living manifestation of unadulterated Commanding Self) decided to take American troops out of Syria in 2019, leaving Erdogan (a demagogue) to move in against the Kurds and gain ground domestically in Turkey, giving Assad (a tyrant) an excuse to come in to help the Kurds to strengthening himself, then encouraging Russian mediation between all and sundry. That diplomacy may seem constructive, but it is a series of convoluted manoeuvres that only temporarily stabilise a very difficult situation but do permit Putin (an arch practitioner of the arts of the ego) to gain global profile. One move, and the manipulators and tyrants gain, while the situation in Syria gets no better.

We are not used to looking at the world like this: that apparent enemies such as ISIS, Assad, Putin and the Israeli extremists share a common trait – that of a lesser humanity, a crude force bent on fragmenting the world for its own purposes. In the Middle East, so far, the Commanding Self has won.

As a colleague told me, "In the region, leaders don't care about prosperity or improvements; they're only interested in survival, and it is only when that is threatened that they will act." This may be all too true, but that is only one possible way of being human – and a poor one at that.

We do need a Commanding Self. Its task is to ensure our survival and basic contentment. In enlightened beings, that is the task it performs; in the rest of us, it can, like a clever parasite, infiltrate and take over our minds to varying degrees.

Our physical and emotional needs are the basic components of that Commanding Self; status, group belonging, and attention are all natural elements of the ego. When our needs are not met well and we begin to worry, overthink, obsess and fantasize about how to get them addressed, we lose perspective and become more easily malleable. This is why manipulators and demagogues create situations involving threat and uncertainty, so they can entangle us in their web. Their Commanding Selves feed off ours and expand mercilessly, and we risk losing any notion of the possibility of a more positive life.

While we all have natural but *limited* needs for status, belonging, intimacy and meaning, it is when they are without end that the Commanding Self grows to huge and devastating proportions. Its appetites are basically infinite; it is our human givens gone rogue – and it is why taming and mastering our political ego is so crucial.

It is only when we can learn to satisfy these needs consciously and intelligently, and to a necessary limit, that the Commanding Self can remain a servant rather than, as it is in the Middle East, a master of our future.

THE MISSING PIECE – REDUX

[God] gave us so many emotions and such strong ones that every human being, even if he is an idiot, is a millionaire in emotions.

– Isaac Bashevis Singer [1]

HERE is a summary of where we have come to before we move forward:

1. There is a hidden, missing piece in our politics. This consists of the basic yet profound motivations behind our individual and group behaviour. These are needs that spur us to survive and flourish, and they are expressed in myriad ways.

2. If these needs are unmet, we are thrust into anxiety and high emotion that thwart all efforts at finding more creative solutions or becoming adaptable. The motivation to satisfy these needs is so powerful that we will do so by <u>any means available</u>, including criminality, extremism, blind ideological and identity projects – or simple opinion-mongering on social media.

3. The inability to satisfy these basic motivations in a balanced way – partly because of the sheer lack of knowledge about them – means that they are prone to manipulation by greedy or malevolent leaders or influencers.

4. These motivations are the basic constituents of our ego, a living system of survival that seeks its satisfaction at all costs, unless tamed. As a reflection of ego, the preservation of self-image can be more important than self-preservation itself. We will not budge easily from its demands, which is why economic sanctions don't work, and conflicts seem intractable.

5. Unless we develop better awareness (and detectors), the problems resulting from these motivations only become apparent *after* the Titanic hits the iceberg: The Arab revolutions, the fall of the Berlin Wall, 9/11, Brexit, Trump (and who knows what else in the future) – all these major events came out of nowhere. Our gaze is on other factors while a dangerous, future builds slowly and silently in the hearts and minds of political actors.

6. You can try to drive nature out, but it will come back in the end. It is our job to ensure that the way needs manifest and are met is useful and constructive.

In Ancient Rome they used to write on tombstones: "NF F NS NC" – *non fui, fui, non sum, non caro.* "I didn't exist, I did exist, I don't exist, I have no cares." We're all ending up in the same place in the end. Although we are all millionaires of emotions, and these emotions can indeed trump facts, the ability to use stoic calm to deal with adversity is one of our greatest capacities. It is important to keep perspective on issues, and it takes calm to do that. People can learn to differentiate between strong feelings and understanding, and to know that the latter may not come *at all* from having feelings about something. Feelings are fickle and untrustworthy friends, and, in the end, it is calm that wins.

Indeed, some NF F NS NC can even win you a war. As a North Vietnamese fighting in the south said, "I showed up (back home) after six years, six years without a letter. For six years, my mother had no idea whether I was alive or dead. My mother cried, but we did not make a scene. Vietnamese are like that."[2]

MAKING THE HUMAN DISAPPEAR

The Feast

After yet another disastrous project that resulted in higher taxes and more hardship imposed on the people, a wise man let it be known at court that he was a master chef. One day he announced a feast at which he would prepare the most delicious new food. The King and all of his advisers were invited.

When the various dignitaries arrived, full of anticipation, the food was presented in great style. But it proved to be disgusting.

"What is this abominable, poisonous mess you are asking us to eat?" cried the outraged guests. "You're making us all sick!"

"This is my latest recipe. I made it up as I went along, putting in at random anything that came to hand if it seemed like a good idea."

"That's absurd!" the King and all his advisors shouted at once. "That's no way to prepare a meal."

"I agree," said the wise one before making a hasty exit, "But I thought it would be interesting, nonetheless, to try out a recipe based on your way of doing things." [1]

WE DON'T attend to matters according to the summary above. We have developed other means, laws, moral codes and police forces to keep our animal spirits at bay. Yet, these old ways may be less and less effective as the world grows in complexity and connectivity while international relations remain a game of one-upmanship, each nation trying to eat up another before being eaten, all now accelerated by cyberwarfare. Before moving on, let us look at these more traditional ways of doing things:

The Blue Light at Erez: The Resort to Security Methods

While working with the United Nations in 2000, I lived in Gaza for a short time. Unlike the locals, I was able to exit the Strip and go to Israel with relative ease through Erez – the crossing point at the northern border. When I first passed through it in the 1990s, it was a typical Israeli security checkpoint, a waiting room with desks and counters, and line-ups leading to young women in uniform who fired questions at you about your intentions towards their country.

I had already experienced many such grillings at Ben Gurion airport but Erez was more mysterious. Sometimes permission to proceed would come quickly, other times not. While waiting for the security system to spin the roulette wheel of your fate, you could step outside and peer beyond the compound of security towers and administrative buildings at the hills of southern Israel.

When I watched Palestinians trying to get in and out of Gaza, I would develop a strong sense of guilt. The workmen who left that morning, suffering through very long line-ups, went through the same agony in the evening. In comparison, as a privileged international, I sailed through with VIP-like treatment.

That was Erez then. I experienced it again in 2005 after the second Intifadah had changed everything. Palestinian suicide bombers had led Israel to take tougher measures to protect its officials. This new Erez was something to behold, for there was no one to be seen. Other than the official who examines identity papers behind bulletproof glass, the rest of your relationship with the security services is barked out through a loud megaphone system.

You first enter a small area barred by metal gates that open and close automatically. Then you are ordered through a loudspeaker to turn around, spread your arms, and disclose what is under your shirt. The commands come in Hebrew and the sound quality is poor because it is broadcast through cheap speakers. If you do not respond, the orders are repeated in Arabic, the incomprehensibility now compounded by the accent of the Israeli shouting the commands.

One time, I saw an elderly Palestinian woman crossing. She froze, confused and intimidated by the orders, the metal gates, and the impersonality of it all. Her paralysis increased as the barks got more vociferous, but she had no idea what to do. She was in sheer terror. Fortunately, she ultimately managed to respond.

Such a humiliating experience is only exacerbated by the lack of any humans around. There is no one to be seen. No doubt this protects Israeli security officials from attack, but it also shows how frighteningly efficient Israelis can be in 'finding solutions' to the Palestinian problem. At Erez, they made the human disappear.

After you're done, there is a long walk under a high stall-like structure. Its arched ceiling is made of plastic that leaks an eerie cold blue light down onto the shoddy surroundings, reflecting just how cold and insensitive we can become in order to survive, or maintain what we have. Erez today is closed except for exceptional cases but, as acts of terror spread across societies and A.I. makes control much easier, its security paradigm has spread, too.

A common answer in today's politics, and in the Middle East especially, is the security response to manage the perception of threat, or simply crush an unruly enemy's ego. There are several strategies to deal with group instincts and Haidt's leaning elephant. The first, popular in the Middle East, is to keep bashing the elephant until it is cowed into submission. Tyrants and security forces do just that to keep any rampaging contained. Saddam Hussein did it to Kurds and Shia, Israelis do it to Palestinians, and Assad does it to rebellious Sunnis. Whipping dogs (and elephants) into line is traditional and time-tested. Elephants may succumb to brute force, but they also have long memories.

Indeed, once 9/11 happened, 'Israeli rules' (security uber alles) overtook Western countries. The US, the mightiest power in the world, took on all the actions that Israelis had specialized in – fences, walls, security checks, hyper-intelligence activity, drones, extra-judicial killings became de rigueur. The blue light at Erez is now effectively everywhere. We have become used to its results: lockdown, pervasive security at airports, security cameras on the street, and a lack of privacy.

The resort to security measures is a natural inclination, and the technology available at our fingertips today permits us to pursue it with greater and greater ease – and the human disappears more and more.[2] The security reaction is at many times necessary, but it *dehumanizes*. Unintended victims will have less human capacity to respond in a crisis, and violence ends up becoming more likely. Indeed, it is surprising that people in the Middle East remain as human as they are given the abuse that they experience.

Tougher security measures mean that resentment festers below the surface, where it 'boils and bubbles' and, like Macbeth's witches, foretells a dark future involving many who today are innocent but who may not remain so, once mistreated. As former Israeli Prime Minister Ehud Barak said, "If I were a

Palestinian at the right age, I would have joined one of the terrorist organizations at a certain stage."[3]

The Law

The traditional and fairly successful way of putting limits on misbehaviour is through abidance with the law, a road that implies fairness and objectivity. Laws are built on the idea of coercing us more fairly into acceptable patterns of behaviour. They're explicit and backed up both by sanction and judges (wise ones, we hope) who can lead us through grey areas of interpretation, when needed. It is why the mantra of 'the rule of law' is often expressed as a cure for bad politics.

However, it does not always work. Belief in institutions and the rule of law is a half measure that may not carry the day in managing unrequited or inflamed emotional needs. Our abstracted institutional and legal world is fragile in the face of a blood-rise of inflamed egos.

For example, in Spain, the central government decided at first to ignore the fact that some Catalans sought independence from Spain. I suppose the Spanish government thought the issue would just go away, or maybe its leaders simply did not know what to do. When the Catalonian regional government held a referendum in 2017 that resulted in a call for independence, the Spanish government's response was to say that it was illegal and unconstitutional. However, Catalonian needs have little to do with law and constitutions. They are about our basic drivers asserting themselves, whether the need for greater economic autonomy, or a sense of historical identity denied. The majority of people in Catalonia probably never wanted to leave Spain, but they needed to have these basic issues of autonomy and status attended to (possibly again and again until they calm down) – not exacerbated by a crude and monolithic reference to law.

We need laws to keep societies coherent, but we also need the wisdom to know when law applies, and when it is less relevant to the question at hand. Indeed, when strong motivations kick in, the law, and its enforcers, can be perceived as the very barrier to getting our needs met, and the result can be further inflammation.

Reputation & Fear of the Almighty

Another method of keeping us in line is highlighted by scientist Dominic Johnson in his book, *God is Watching You: How the Fear of God Makes Us Human.* He explains how the threat of punishment by the supernatural is key for building an ordered and successful society. It seems it is more effective than law or secular instruments in enforcing order. No wonder we have the expression to 'put the fear of God' in someone. This is well exemplified in the words spoken by 66-year old Jorge Ortiz Diaz, a government employee, after assisting with rescues during an earthquake in Mexico: "It's like Sodom and Gomorrah, like God is angry at us. Now is the moment when solidarity begins."[4] Whether with the Ten Plagues or the Biblical Flood, God could threaten what no human could.

Of course, this does not always play out benignly. After the 2004 Indian Ocean earthquake and tsunami, an advisor to the Saudi Justice Minister expressed the belief that nations were destroyed for lying and sinning, and another sheikh believed that the tsunami was Allah's revenge at Bangkok's corruption.[5] Nice guy.

Johnson is an evolutionary biologist and his thesis is that belief in supernatural punishment favoured natural selection because it diminished selfish behaviour and heightened group cooperation: the ego tamed. He points out that the fear of God makes us reflect more on our actions, even when we are alone –

it's between us and the Lord.[6] The threat of supernatural punishment is more effective at making us cooperate than more legal and social means.[7]

Another related form of coercion and putting limits on basic drives is the power of reputation. Jonathan Haidt, author of *The Righteous Mind*, opines that the most important principle for designing an ethical society is to make sure everyone's reputation is *on the line all the time*. The most crucial stimulus to the development of the social virtues is the fact that people are passionately concerned with the praise and blame of their fellow men; it's the more subtle but effective whip.

This organic method, developed over millions of years, can also turn out to be ineffective. In the Middle East, there is often a false obedience to reputation that often involves cultivating a good repute while trying to get away with whatever one can under the table, behind one's back, or even directly in someone else's face, i.e. hypocrisy is rampant. In the West, reputation is also having a hard time. Donald Trump eviscerated it by demonstrating that unacceptable words and actions are not an obstacle to gaining and keeping power, and a Western individual's right to be anything he or she wants or claims to be, without challenge, has 'trumped' societal restraints based on reputation.

Indeed, the opposite has set in, the more foulmouthed or pornographic one is, the more attention one gets, especially through social media.

Reputation is slipping and misappropriated in the West, and is hollowed out in the Middle East, and the result is a general lack of control and restraint. If the rule of law and reputation slip simultaneously, then we will think more frequently of coercion and oppression as a recourse to maintain order.

It may not be a coincidence that our world today fluctuates between a liberal free for all and increasing authoritarianism –

the more traditional and organic methods of keeping us in line are slipping.

The Method: Analysis

Another approach is the classic 'Western' game of trying to impose some order onto the 'irrational' through negotiations, institutions, techniques, maps, and rational argument. Useful as it may be, the work of think tanks and technocrats across the world often ignore the emotional element, and therefore fall short – there's an elephant in the way. (This is the equivalent of cognitive behaviour methods in psychology; all good on the thinking front but it does not address the emotional needs).

In such cases, we don't try to tame the political animal, we simply ignore it in favour of 'talk' and the stimulation that arises out of endless analysis. This has become a 21st century specialty: over-analysis, an endless stream of re-presentation of politics that takes us away from the real world, putting in its place: articles, tweets, reports and opinion. These often ignore the live dynamics that are creating most of the havoc.[8]

Think tanks have proliferated, many of them doing good work, providing information and pointing at the dynamics. However, many of these reports are abstracted and flat representations of a living and much more dynamic reality. The richesse of analysis today is because we value words and interesting thinking, more than results in the real world.

For example, the World Economic Forum Risk Report depicts the variables that affect the workings of society and their interrelationships in an image of a thirteen pointed star. At each point are real factors such as the weakening of international governance, the growing middle class in emerging economies, and rising income disparity – all interlinked in a clever and geometric way. The star is almost symmetrical, somewhat beautiful, and, on a good day, can even make some sense – maybe. But using this interconnected, multivariable map defies human capacity and judgment. It requires machine-like computational power – the linkages are too many and even with the most powerful computer involved, there is one small piece missing: the human being in the whole affair.

In the real world, behind every single variable shown and involved in every relation depicted there is a human being. The moods, priorities and motivations of real individuals may upset the whole apple cart, or make it work very oddly. How dedicated are people to their jobs? Do they have enough emotional spare capacity to think of others, or to do their jobs properly? All these factors are more likely to decide success or failure, yet they are assumed, not considered.

No matter how well we map our world, attractive images or otherwise, it is the active agent, the human being, that creates the interconnectivities in the real world. It is also the human being that creates the computer that can possibly manage it, yet we often forget to understand, or even consider, our own 'software.'

"Politics as Usual" – The Rubik's Cube

A larger issue than all of the above is simply the nature of "politics as usual." This involves real and difficult considerations of evolving factors but it is also an endless Rubik's Cube of manoeuvring. Most of it is aimed at protecting ourselves from loss or maximizing gain, or reacting impulsively to change i.e. the ego's very finely-honed equations. We can look at the Israel-Palestine conflict to get a sense of the complexity and near-miraculous alignment of forces needed to find a solution.

In any real deal, Israelis would have to let go of land in the West Bank, as well as parts of Jerusalem, which for security reasons or historical attachments many Israelis are not yet prepared to do. Taking the road of peace may create conflict between Israelis, which politicians calculate as more costly in the short term than fighting their enemy. Therefore, for some, holding on to that land is more important than peace with the Palestinians.

On the other hand, Palestinians are oppressed and they do not want to recognize the validity of their enemy's cause. Israelis think that recognizing Palestinian suffering implies an admission of an 'original sin' in the creation of their state. Israelis' self-image as the primary victims of history would be threatened, and prevents them from recognizing their adversaries more fully.

The powerful underlying motives are also expressed politically in ways that people quite often get married to. The political formulation of the need becomes more important than having the need itself met. People come to see the forms as reality itself, unaware of the more fundamental, underlying drivers. This can result in inflexibility and uncompromising political positions.

For example, for Palestinians, the righting of a past wrong has been formulated politically as the *right of return*, based on UN General Assembly Resolution 194, which states that refugees can go back to their homes if they are willing to live at peace with their neighbours. This was written in 1951, and the local circumstance has changed somewhat since then, including the presence of highways and skyscrapers where once there were homes. However, for Palestinians, 'the right of return' remains incontestable. (For Israelis, to recognise this risks the Jewish nature of their state). Refugees' needs can possibly be met in other ways than the right of return.

For Israelis, the idea of a *Jewish state* has become the formulation for the recognition of their presence. However, Arabs are loath to use this language because it legitimizes the actions taken in 1948 by the Zionists, and because of concerns about the many non-Jewish residents of Israel. However, there may be other forms that can satisfy Israelis than the proposed one. The two sides are more tied to such political *formulations* of needs than the needs themselves.

Both sides have red lines, or principles, that bind their people together – and then bind politicians' hands. For both sides, the risks to political survival of an imperfect deal with uncertain long-term gains make the calculation seem not worth it – at least for now. It is a rare leader who is willing to go against the ingrained habits of his society and break new ground that would effectively humanize the other side – and this is politics as usual.

Indeed, these are only some of the considerations involved. We still have internal competition between forces inside each country, rivalries within parties, electoral factors, relations with global powers, and how the weather and family life affect the moods of decision-makers on any given day.

Is there any way to better manage this bouillabaisse?

All of the above methods may be at times necessary, but they are all coercive, and they stunt the possibility of a full and satisfied human being appearing on the scene – they are still fully in the realm of the ego.

Politics are the arena where we manage and give order to society by controlling and accessing resources and power. It is a kind of privileged zone, which is why it fascinates. But the availability of power, status and resources also means it lures those greedy for such qualities, and the ignorant citizen is left prone and vulnerable to becoming cannon-fodder. We use the rule of law, institutions and cultural norms to control such excesses. Yet, it may be worth remembering the words of Ralph Waldo Emerson as we move forward:

"Fear, Craft, and Avarice
Cannot rear a State.
Out of dust to build
What is more than dust." [9]

It may be time to look for a new concept for politics and to manage our affairs in a different way. We may want to reconceive our politics to put the human front and centre. If we prioritize the needs of citizens, then the whole structure, indeed possibly even the accumulation of resources and power that so attracts, may be different.

MUTUAL NEEDS SATISFACTION

Enemies are often former or potential friends who have been denied – or think that they have been denied – something.

– Idries Shah, *Reflections* [1]

ANTHROPOLOGISTS and psychologists have found that basic needs not only cannot be ignored, as in Oslo, but they are also not 'tradable,' as in a marketplace. They need to be satisfied in and of themselves. Jeremy Ginges, professor at the New School for Social Research in New York, carried out research showing how we process different values in distinct parts of our brain. He labelled these non-tradable 'sacred values' – ones that we don't wish to put on the bargaining table. "Attempts to trade them backfire and may cause the sides to become infuriated and dig in."[2]

Today, as we have seen, in politics, we pursue advantage, *our* advantage. But there are several studies that demonstrate that progress can be made by chipping away at the ego through mutual needs satisfaction. Scott Atran and Jeremy Ginges have indicated that extremists, the largest problem on both sides, are more likely to accept deals where the enemy makes symbolic but difficult gestures, whereas transactional, business-like negotiations favoured by the West will backfire. As in the case of *aberu* with Iran, progress on these innate human needs could lead to talks on more material issues – not the other way around. Some large-scale surveys have shown that if Palestinians can acknowledge the Holocaust as a source of victimization for Israeli Jews, Israelis become readier to accept responsibility for Palestinian suffering.[3]

Polling in 2018 supports this approach. Khalil Shikaki's Palestinian Center for Policy and Survey Research and Dalia Scheindlin, a fellow at the Century Foundation and who is also affiliated with Tel Aviv University, reported that less than half of Palestinians and Israelis support two states, but that acts of good faith could make a big difference. "If Israelis would recognize the Naqba"—the "disaster," when seven hundred and fifty thousand Palestinians went into exile as a result of the 1948 war—and "Palestinians would make clear that, with peace, Israelis could visit the Temple Mount—the Haram al-Sharif—then almost half of the Israeli Jews opposed to two states, and about forty per cent of the Palestinians, would change their minds." [4] Imperfect, but not bad at all for a conflict that has lingered for a very long time. Dealing with innate human needs first is crucial, it calms us down.

As we saw in the case of the USA-Iran nuclear deal, starting with *aberu* before *maslahat* helped, i.e. putting first things first. What if negotiations between the Israelis and Palestinians also began only by recognizing clearly the basic and key needs on both sides *first* in a process of mutual needs satisfaction?

What if Israelis first recognized that *Palestinians need proper autonomy, status and legitimacy through the establishment of a Palestinian state as well as a recognition of their past suffering.* The last bit is key: the Palestinian people have suffered from the creation of Israel, even if this was the result of another people seeking a haven to end their own suffering (such contradictions can exist). If Israel recognizes this, much Palestinian agony over having become a discarded people, without status for over seven decades, can begin to ease. Israelis today are also more powerful than the Palestinians, therefore, without negating Israelis' historical trauma, if they took the first sincere steps to ameliorate the Palestinians' conditions, they might be surprised by the positive attitudes engendered in their enemy.

What if Palestinians could recognize that *Israel needs to live in security and safety and to be accepted in the region* and that *Jews have a longstanding heritage in the Middle East and the Holy Land, and that they are today part of the region, in the state of Israel.* What if they could say that, *despite the past, Palestinians look forward to living beside them in peace and security in two states.* This would attend to the Israeli need for belonging and status in the region, as well as the need for security.

Simultaneous recognition of needs may be difficult because, after half a century of Israeli occupation of the Palestinians, the distrust is high on both sides, and the memories long.

Yet, an agreement that begins and is founded on two foundational statements made by high quality leaders would lower emotion, change perceptions, dissolving the old variables, and help in creating the context for finding new and more positive ways of meeting needs. The elements of the ego would calm down and we enter the green zone where progress is more likely to be made.[5] Emotions on both sides could sufficiently calm down to deal concretely with the many complex issues between them.

My guess is that, if this new approach were taken, there would be an outcry from 20 percent of the population on both sides, as the accumulated frustrations, false expectations and fantasies of decades are triggered and exposed – there is no ignoring the build-up of old patterns. This spasm of emotional and physical violence would be difficult to contain but, if understood as the outpouring of the pain from the past, not an indicator of the future, it could end positively. If leaders and systems could hold the rocky road for a year or two – admittedly a tough feat – all might well settle down, as basic needs start to be met and appreciated by the 80 percent who want more normal lives. This does require real political leadership.

In my business, such steps are often called confidence-building measures (or CBMs): actions, such as opening a checkpoint or trading prisoners, aimed at calming the parties down. So, in a way, I am proposing the ultimate CBMs, ones that might actually work because they are attending to the core of what the sides care about, what is driving them to fight and die.

In the case of Israel and Palestine, there *are* practical solutions, whether it is the Arab Peace Initiative,[6] two states, one state, a confederation, or everything in between – the possibilities are many. What will decide the health of the result will be the underlying relationship between the sides and the recognition that there must be *mutual needs satisfaction*: both sides need to have their deeper human needs attended to at the level of the 'base camp,' putting first things first.

It is to this end, and to better manage our sea of emotions, that I have set up, with the aid of likeminded others, an international initiative called The Conciliators Guild, to spread many of the ideas in this book into the political sphere, so we can all up our game, and manage our challenges better over the long term.[7] And, at the Conciliators Guild, I am currently involved in a diplomatic initiative that depicts the basic needs of the key countries in the Middle East and looks at them all together, in one context – unlike the usual habit of focusing on an interest or a country, here or there.

This effort stresses that we have to focus on the core needs of the critical countries shaping the region (Turkey, Saudi Arabia,

Israel, Iran and Egypt) and not get lost in how they get them met, which is often through counterproductive processes such as Iran's offensive defence, Israeli pre-emptive strikes, or Turkish forays into northern Syria. These approaches resolve short-term problems but create larger ones in the future by breeding resentment and a desire for revenge.

Regional mutual needs satisfaction in the Middle East is the way to get the core needs that create conflict calmed down enough to have mutual regional security – and a solid foundation for moving forward.

PRAGMATIC AND CREATIVE:
A MORE INTELLIGENT CITIZENRY

"Freedom of speech and freedom of action are meaningless without freedom to think."

– Bergan Evans, *The Natural History of Nonsense*[1]

WE CAN move beyond our old-fashioned ways of restraining that ego, (law, security and institutions), and slowly but surely gain political freedom that is driven by greater knowledge that will naturally encourage self-restraint. The real precursor to the freedom to act and speak is the freedom to think properly. Political freedom increases when we are not in the thrall of a manipulator, getting our needs met through an extreme group or cult, or following our well-worn political opinions. Here are some other ways to deal with politics in a sensible and, ultimately, more human manner:

Practise Pragmatism not ideology. On a rare sunny day in the UK, I walked out to see the gardener trimming the hedges, and I thought to myself, this is exactly what taming the political ego is about. It is about working with, but limiting the basic drives so they don't grow gargantuan and take on a life of their own that we can no longer control.

I began a conversation with him, and he had that common wisdom that one can often find among people who are not heavily involved in politics. He told me that he had never voted because he never believed in 'left' or 'right.' He thinks the right is trying to keep their money for themselves and away from the middle, and the left taking from the middle for the poor. "Neither left nor right" made sense to me – it was beyond ideologies, and the middle, where he belonged, implied balance and sense. And, this is a necessary way to look at matters in order to get constructive things done, rather than go on an ideological trip.[2] There is possibly not one issue in the Middle East that does not have a pragmatic solution. However ego, and its political maidservant, ideology, are directly in the way.

Think about creative ways to help people meet their needs. Extremists, unless they are psychopaths, are not evil nor, necessarily, economically disadvantaged. They are, in the main, young men looking for excitement, glory, belonging and meaning in their lives, and some of the bad guys deliver it by the truckload. They want something to fight for – why not be open to creating ways to fight for good.

A useful example is that of Gulalai Ismail, her sister Saba and a group of friends who set up the Seeds of Peace network to change the lives of young women in Khyber Pakhtunkhwa, North-West Pakistan. They focused on women's role in society and trained young activists to challenge violent extremism. Twenty-five people have been trained and over 150 have since applied to join this movement of activists against religious and political extremism.[3] It is a clever way to counter the illness by getting potential extremists to fight extremism. Is there such a shortage of challenges in the world for young people to focus on, to enable them to feel somehow 'heroic' while doing something positive?[4]

Those responsible, in governments and their bureaucracies, are often the least capable of seeing matters in this way. Such organizations are defined by risk-aversion, and a desire to keep their jobs. A fear of creativity, and decisions made by committee, are not likely to come up with the necessary bold and creative answers.

Yet, sometimes, we can see a more human-based approach in action. In Arhus, Denmark, approaches were successfully implemented to deal with violent extremism. When radicalized individuals who had travelled to join ISIS returned, the Danes in Arhus did not take away their passports. Instead, "They made it clear to citizens of Denmark who had travelled to Syria that they were welcome to come home, and that, when they did, they would receive help with going back to school, finding an apartment, meeting with a psychiatrist or a mentor, or whatever they needed to fully integrate back into society. ... They [had expected] to be treated harshly. ... That kind of shock opens people's minds to maybe they were wrong about their society that they perceived as their enemy. It opens a possible window into rethinking and re-evaluating."[5]

The Arhus experiment was not a one-off. Researchers have found that being on the receiving end of an *unexpected altruistic act* can have a strong positive impact on one's subsequent view of life. Three quarters of those [surveyed] who had experienced unexpected altruism said it had strongly changed their view of life. The stronger the experience the more it generated positive outlooks on relationships and a sense of self-esteem.[6] Maybe some of the extremists need to be shocked by the upside of being human, an altruistic act that is without condition. An unusual thought.

. . .

Be Machiavellian: Don't vote for or support egotists, even if you love their brand. Despite protestations otherwise, or loud claims of virtue, many enter into politics mainly to join an elite club. Their eye is on the prestige, status, attention, and sometimes the money, far away from the common weal. They enter into politics in order to be above the crowd, the common man, and his 'commonness' – not to serve.

Today, this gap between club and weal is exacerbated by globalization and the rise of megacities that elites flock to, distancing them even further from any link to their citizens. Social contracts weaken an inability to control global money flows: "Money flows across frontiers, but laws do not."[7]

Only a sincere desire to render public service will provide the incentive to learn how human beings function and to begin to use that in a healthy fashion. The desire to be a member of an elite club of power seekers will not.

For many, the problem remains our leaders, for they are responsible.

How are we to deal with a world with such a low bar for leaders, and rely on gangsters, robbers and charmers in positions that affect our future? Sadly, the problem is even worse than all that. "Taken as a whole, the ruling groups are more talented intellectually and more deranged mentally than the ruled population," said sociologist Pitirim Sorokin.[8] Power attracts the deranged and twists them even further.

Indeed, power and wealth corrupt in unexpectedly mundane ways, as research has shown. People who feel powerful are less likely to show empathy; in experiments, when wealthy people watched a video about children with cancer, they showed fewer physiological signs of empathy. Wealthy subjects were more likely to cheat in games involving small cash stakes and to take candies from a jar that was designated for children. Wealth and power don't seem to breed much good, the researchers concluded.[9]

In such a circumstance, some advice comes from an unexpected quarter. One of the most famous political philosophers of history, Niccolò Machiavelli, had a few things to say about power, and gave his name to the art of self-serving political manipulation. In his book, *The Prince*, he told rulers that the way men actually were was so different from how they should be that only a fool seeking his downfall would abandon 'what is for what should be.' He is notorious for his clear-headed advice on how to govern without mercy.

However, Erica Benner, a professor of political philosophy, has analyzed Machiavelli's ideas in new ways, and she says that the Italian philosopher actually aimed to have citizens become more aware of their leaders' games. She believes that he insinuated this into *The Prince* and, indeed, when nearing his death, Machiavelli said that he had wanted to teach citizens "the way to hell, so they can steer clear of it." Although commonly viewed as rulers' best friend, "he was warning citizens of the 16th-century Republic of Florence not to be fooled by cunning leaders," Benner argues.[10][11]

"Sharpen (your) senses and notice the ways in which power is abused and the ways in which leaders overstep and stealthily strip away freedoms and standards," Machiavelli wrote. "You have to pay attention when leaders start making arguments designed to pit one group of citizens against another, when they claim they need more power and have to limit the courts, when they start undermining the rule of law for the sake of expediency."[12] He was basically telling citizens to develop some form of X-ray vision to see through their leaders' egos better.

Citizens need to become responsible for their choice of leaders, and if they do listen to these warnings, the term 'Machiavellian' may come to have new meaning.

A wily leader cannot manipulate a more intelligent citizen. Imagine a leader who does not promise you heaven, nor plays with your fears of hell, nor indulges your false pride, and you are beginning to look in the right direction. It may also be useful to remember the hypnotic manipulation described earlier, and snap out of it once recognized.

Elites and leaders are far from all bad; many are dedicated to excellence and to improving their society. We can help them along by being better citizens. We would not choose a lawyer, doctor or accountant whose mental health is suspect. *Maybe one day we will also learn to extend that judgment to our leaders.*

The tough work ahead is to improve emotional understanding so that when asked to make choices between self-serving politicians or service-oriented statesmen and women, we know the difference. Each of us is the last line of defence against predation and folly.

FIND A MIRROR

I proclaimed peace to the creatures of God, and never called for war against them. But I did take up arms against my ego, without ever negotiating any ceasefire.

– Kharraqani [1]

WHEN LOOKING at the hills of the West Bank or the deserts of Egypt, flashes often would come to my mind of the Old Testament prophets. They had spoken of a need for a deeper kind of resilience to guide us through tough times, of the development of strong character in the face of the turbulence and savagery of life. They also spoke of consequences for our actions, a reality that is all too often simply denied. Today, we often feel others must bear the responsibility for our difficulties, and that life is a series of entitlements – or that we are simply here for our amusement.

The ravages of the Commanding Self in the Middle East today show that the prophets were right. If we don't build up an immunity to our baser selves, and develop a kind of overall intelligence to manage our way through the challenges of life, it can all go wrong. Nowhere is this more applicable than in politics.

"Institutions only exist *because civilization has failed,*" said writer and scholar Idries Shah.[2] All our great institutions, from bureaucracies to the church to universities, constrain and coerce us into certain limits on our behaviour, but they remain "what barbed wire is to containing animals." Institutions are only in place because most people can't be relied on to be honest, fair and humane towards one another, or act from a body of real knowledge about how to behave.[3] Can we evolve more towards having greater 'internal control' over ourselves, rather than being coerced by external factors, as we saw in the last section?

This book began with this verse from Ovid,

"And the first age was Gold,
Without laws, without laws' enforcers
This age understood and obeyed
What had created it,
Listening deeply, man kept faith with the source."

It is unlikely we will ever have a society without any laws, but we can try to maximize the quality of citizens and their capacities and, so, minimize the degree of 'barbed wire.' It may be time, indeed *the* time, to admit that the answers may lie in a place that no one really wants to look, practices no longer strongly encouraged, such as self-discipline, patience, self-reflection, greater knowledge, and restraining our impulses (yawn!), i.e. being civilized, or what those Middle Eastern and other prophets and philosophers were angling for all along: a more intelligent human being, and therefore, a more intelligent citizen whose judgment results from personal development and a flexible mind that can also see the needs of others.

This seems difficult to do because we are unpractised.

Studies have however shown that placing a real mirror in front of people improves their moral decision-making, and it may be wise to remember that *the summary of the advice of all prophets is this; Find yourself a mirror.* A good look in it, and it will almost certainly be clear that our problems are a result of blindness, greed, or an incorrect, or incorrectly developed, self-image.

Ironically, we may be going in the opposite direction. We may end up in some ways relying on an advanced version of all of the forms of barbed wire discussed previously: a Big Brother form of artificial intelligence that provides coercion, is legal, plays on our sense of reputation, at least in the virtual realm, and even mimics the great supernatural eye in the sky, watching us all the time. It may even be more effective than all of the above coercive methods combined, because it is more subtle, and less visible. However, this is a step towards life as a virtual imprisonment, a sheep pen for human beings, with little room for upside.

The better way forward comprises using that mirror a little better, recognizing that we are deeply emotional creatures, learn to master that, and develop a calm way forward. By doing so, we will be released from a series of veils, many composed of intense emotions, that obstruct a view of a larger context that is almost certainly less conflictual.

We may also find that others share the human givens with us, and we have much in common. With enough sincere effort, that mirror may indeed become a doorway onto a new outlook, where the world, filled with foibles as it is, has many challenges but fewer enemies that we currently construe. Once we open up to the needs of others, then mutual needs satisfaction and mutual respect can ensue.

MAKING THE HUMAN REAPPEAR

Who or what can give me the power of transforming a mirror into a doorway?

– Dag Hammarskjold [1]

WE ALL LIVE in contexts of constant interaction with others. Whether in families, nations or between nations, we are bound to be in both friction and harmony with each other. The need and lives of others are infinitely intertwined with our own – trouble is bound to happen. We need other ways to make the human reappear, or to prevent its disappearance in the first place.

I have had direct experience that difficult human shifts can happen once awareness of human needs occurs. I was privy to a multi-year dialogue between someone linked to Hamas and an Israeli. During the talks, they both suffered at times from a fear that deep existential and emotional needs would not be met by the other, and that they would, even in this dialogue, metaphorically be forgotten and devalued as individuals and as a people, and thrown into the dustbin of history. Beyond the armies and rockets was this very human fact, and it applied to both sides – even the more powerful Israeli side.

Early on, they came to the table with mental walls, defences, aggressive postures and attempts to show that they were beyond manipulation or, as Israelis put it, beyond being a 'friar,' the term for a sucker in Hebrew. But, over time, I saw that deeper sense of vulnerability surface, and a kind of fresh willingness to consider new ideas. Slowly, they began to see the other as a human being, not just a threat.

Over three years of discussions, a considerable degree of understanding developed between the two men, especially once they saw that the essence of their humanity was not going to be completely denied. At various points in their talks, the penny dropped and they began to see that the other had real, common needs behind the demands. They began to see a simple human expression that they could understand and shared.

In a way, they did become friends once they realized that the other was a mirror of their own needs, "you are like me." I could see this recognition on their face when it occurred; they looked at each other more plainly and sincerely.

Both were well connected to their respective systems and, several times, they took constructive ideas to their leaders. However, those leaders calculated the political cost to be too high, and did not take the ideas on. There were also complications regarding the choreography or sequencing of steps each side would take, again driven by leaders' assessments of whether the ideas could be absorbed by their people – or, possibly more crucially, make the leaders politically vulnerable. Brave and sincere leaders do matter: the opportunity was lost. [2]

If we increase our capacity to manage ourselves and our behaviour towards others, this would add up to politics being a bit more human, and 'humanized.' The hidden dimension cuts to the heart of the problems in our politics, it may also be the heart of our solutions. It may well be the entry ticket for achieving a humanity that is more 'whole,' and less fragmented.

PART VI

TRANSFORMING OUR GROUP MIND

Souls which recognize one another congregate together.
Those which do not, argue with one another.

– Saying of the Prophet Mohammed in Idries Shah's,
  Caravan of Dreams [1]

"HE NEEDED TIME"

The kind of man required for universalism could not be more contrary to our present man, devoted solely to himself and indifferent to the destiny of his fellow men...he is still conditioned by territorial frontiers, racial prejudices, political trends and religious ideas...To reach universalism man must undergo a radical change....he must be able to cover a wider and more complex panorama, to rise above the differences and to work for the common destiny, an eminently social man...

– Giovanna de Garayalde, *Jorge Luis Borges: Sources and Illumination* [1]

IN 1521, at the battle of Tenochtitlan, the Aztecs put up their last defence against Cortes and his conquering Spanish force. They constructed a great paper serpent into which they poured all the spiritual and magical power of the universe. They were certain that this would kill the Spaniards, and like an ultimate Doomsday Bomb, make them, and the universe, disappear as well. The Spaniards destroyed the paper serpent with their swords and the Aztec last stand was over. [2]

If I was to point to one issue where we need to evolve politically, it would be our group-ego, our tribes, no matter whether they are ideological, national, religious, or otherwise. Faced with powerful challenges today, we may continue to resort to our version of the paper serpent, repeating old mechanisms of survival, including tribalism and 'cult thinking,' which are our instinctive responses to threat. And, these may end up as the very cause of our demise – the Aztecs were also certain their serpent would work.

A closer look at the group identity factor would seem imperative.

In January, 2016, two American Muslims, a man and a woman, stood up at a Trump rally wearing yellow stars, as Jews were forced to wear under the Nazis. They were booed out of the arena, and their protest triggered a wave of racism and tribalism. The woman, Rose Hamid, told the CNN news channel that she "came to the rally to let Trump supporters see what a Muslim looks like." She stood silently holding a T-shirt that displayed the words "I Come In Peace."[3] As she was being ejected, Trump commented on Hamid: "There is hatred against us that is unbelievable. It's their hatred; it's not our hatred." This is little different from the Jewish lawyer in Toronto telling me his people were being exterminated while Israeli tanks were rolling through Palestinian Jenin. Our tribal fixations – forms of self-centered mind – can invert reality, and see upside down as normal in its effort to preserve a certain vision.

Today, we have invented new ways of mismanaging group identity. In 2015, German Chancellor Angela Merkel made a bold move, and permitted hundreds of thousands of refugees, many of them Syrians, to enter Germany. Her 'moral' decision seemed right; she alleviated their immediate suffering and provided a haven in a wealthy nation, also providing her country with needed labour. She touched on the core of many of our political controversies, the stranger among us, and performed a heroic act, partly in atonement of her country's history. However, she seems to have misjudged the impact on her nation.

Patrick Moreau, a researcher at the Centre National de la Recherche Scientifique in France describes her action as a turning point: "Since then, immigration and its perceived threat to national identity have been key factors to understand shifts in European politics."[4] Right wing parties have begun to rise in Germany and centre parties begin to tack right to manage that extreme.[5] "Germany and other countries ... have carried out...reforms (in housing, jobs transport, as in Macron's France) yet they still have experienced a rise in populism,"[6] said Dutch political scientist Cas Mudde. Economic insecurity is at play but a 'cultural clash' is the stronger factor, seeding division and strife.[7]

New York Times columnist Ross Douthat has said, "Much of post-1960s liberal politics ... has been an experiment in cutting Western societies loose from those foundations, set to the tune of John Lennon's 'Imagine.' No heaven or religion, no countries or borders or parochial loyalties of any kind – these are often the values of the centre-left and the far left alike, of neoliberals hoping to manage global capitalism and neo-Marxists hoping to transcend it. Unfortunately, the values of 'Imagine' are simply not sufficient to the needs of human life. People have a desire for solidarity (read, group identity) that cosmopolitanism does not satisfy, immaterial interests that redistribution cannot meet, a yearning for the sacred that secularism cannot answer."[8]

As much as I liked the song "Imagine" when I was 15, it was not the way to go. Come to think of it, I did not even believe it when I was 15. It points to an ideal, but no understanding of how to get there, nor an idea of the obstacles on the way.

Many of the problematic populist reactions in Europe and elsewhere are the result of too much diversity, implemented too quickly. But this is a hard pill for the 'open-minded' to swallow. As Lev Gumilev stated about our identity-passion, "With all due respect, the West does not understand it."[9] What he really means is that liberals, like me, do not understand it.

The problem with tribalism is not only when we run with it without thought (death by identity), but also when we simply ignore it. The free spirit of the 1960s, Woodstock and 'Imagine,' is pleasant, we are stardust, we are golden, but not quite yet – we need more learning to get there.

The roots of the liberal outlook and the ensuing problem may be exactly in an overemphasis on the individual, and not our natural need to be part of an organic collective, i.e. a culture. As economist Todd Buchholz said in *The Price of Prosperity*, if there is no national identity to make people feel part of a larger group, then one result is that narcissism will set in and the individual will twist in his sense of personal supremacy.[10] (Welcome to social media, cancel culture, and a world of untamed ego). The political animal is now everywhere.

He and psychologist Jonathan Haidt come to the same conclusion. "Where religion atrophies, family weakens and patriotism ebbs; other forms of group identity inevitably assert themselves. It is not a coincidence that identity politics are particularly potent on elite college campuses, the most self-consciously post-religious and post-nationalist of institutions; nor is it a coincidence that recent outpourings of campus protest and activism and speech policing and sexual moralizing so often resemble religious revivalism."[11]

A fragmented culture, such as many Western models today, held together by consumerism and law, with little organic culture providing belonging and meaning, is a dangerous thing. It can even affect the migrants so eager for the Western economic cornucopia. Mexican immigrants' level of psycholog- ical disturbance rises with the time they spend in the USA. It is not only that they do not fit into the culture, America has become 'inorganic,' a torn cultural fabric that is being shredded further daily, or replaced by a digital matrix of questionable satisfaction.[12]

Indeed, managing this factor is not a specialty of today's elites. In *The Road to Somewhere*, David Goodhart moves beyond the classical left–right split in politics and demonstrates how the UK is today divided into two 'tribes': *Somewheres*, who are rooted in a specific community and usually socially conservative and *Anywheres*, mobile and more liberal-minded individuals. Anywheres tend to dominate the elites in many countries. However, their ignorance of the social values of their *Somewhere* compatriots, and of the power of cultural identity, results in divisive politics, a new kind of Them and Us. This division helps explain developments such as Brexit, and is echoed in the US in the cleavage between red and blue states. Critically, Goodhart also points out that most of these motivations are operating below the surface, and they resurface easily through uncontrolled or misdirected political reactions.

Goodhart witnessed a European discussion about the refugee crisis in 2015. Delegates thought that population movements from African and East European countries with a youth bulge to offset ageing Western European countries was a 'win-win.' In such a technocratic assessment, no thought was given to how the populations of host countries would react at the level of more basic instincts and identity.[13]

Anywheres like systems of multiculturalism and pluralism to dilute identity urges, but they short-change the power of the identity factor. On Euro bills, there are images of generic gothic doorways and medieval bridges. These images do not refer to any specific bridge or doorway in Europe, they are abstractions put there by Euro-technocrats out of fear of excluding some group or triggering a dark memory from European history, in other words, out of fear of identity. The images do not have any intrinsic meaning to any nationality, they just look generally European, and attempt to skirt national appetites and triggers.

We can also see this ignorance of identity operate more globally. In 2017, the United Nations announced a Global Compact for Migration. This attempts to regulate and put some order into the reality that globalization (in all its forms – technological, transportation and informational) tempts and permits people to move from one place to another, usually from a poorer to a wealthier place in order to work. The UN takes this current reality as its starting point for rules and agreements that are for the mutual benefit of all involved: host countries, migrants' countries of origin, and the migrants themselves. The compact tries to find a balance between state interdependency and traditional national sovereignty.

The possibility that diversity and mixing too rapidly may trigger various degrees of xenophobia in the host populations is mentioned; however, it is given short shrift in comparison to the needs of refugees and migrants. Consideration of the emotional health and circumstances of the host populations, often directly related to identity, is not fully addressed, nor in fact truly seized as an issue.

Back in the Middle East, some Arabs are believers in rights and institutions. Many of these traditional leftists harken back to developments in European history and point to the need for a strong, centralized and secular state to make citizens feel part of a larger entity – they would like the Euro bill. They see the need to dilute sectarian identities into a larger, national cause. Their intent may be noble but the fact that their countries disintegrate into badly fragmented identity zones too readily does not help their case.

At a meeting on the conflict in Yemen, one of the Yemeni participants explained that, in crisis, everyone ran to their 'real identities,' which were at most at the level of the governorate, certainly not the national. A European diplomat familiar with the country confirmed to me that little could be done to help Yemen because the real issues were hidden to Western eyes or to any kind of high-level diplomacy. They were tribal, local and inaccessible to work developed in the diplomatic stratosphere.

Indeed, we may want to heed the words of Mohammad Ali Jinnah, the founder of Pakistan, that Hindus and Muslims are "as divergent today as ever and cannot at any time be expected to transform themselves into one nation merely by means of subjecting them to a democratic constitution and holding them forcibly together by [the] unnatural and artificial methods of British Parliamentary statutes."[14]

Liberalism, says Haidt, "tends to overreach, change too many things too quickly, and reduce stock of moral capital inadvertently."[15] Diversity can trigger alienation and make people more racist unfortunately by emphasizing differences. A balance is needed; all sides of the equation need to be attended to, migration due to globalization, the capacities of the host country, and the identity reflexes of the host as well.

All peoples need to have a sense of belonging to a living culture, a tradition that helps us make sense of the world, and give it order and meaning. The bureaucrats' solutions often fall short, mainly because they are not fully aware of the force they are dealing with. The classic Western response of building better institutions may be a start, but not enough. Much greater awareness of the identity factor and its management may be crucial.

The irony is that, although the UN does not get this, my Bulgarian taxi driver in Oxfordshire does. He told me that his country of origin is not really ready for migrants. Although they can absorb a few, Bulgarians are too concerned about their own circumstances to happily take in strangers and foreigners. If local populations are not prepared for an influx of migrants, or the incoming numbers are too large or arrive too rapidly, and the infrastructure (e.g. in the form of enough homes, schools, capacity in public services) cannot quickly be expanded to cope, chaos can spread to the host countries as well. They will react negatively to large numbers of migrants, and their resentment will be further heightened if the new arrivals are given housing and other services paid for by the EU. How many people in Brussels are considering the reaction of the average Bulgarian when planning migration policy? If he can get it right, using simple common sense, you would think well-educated elites might as well.

We can sum up the situation as follows:

If we enter into the hive switch, unaware of its dangers and implications, including the cult mind, as right-wing conservatives risk doing, we can be taken for quite a ride that might include war, conquest and defeat, or simply misery.

If we ignore the identity factor, as progressive-liberals sometimes do, we lose the possibility of creating trust and contentment in our lives, and create new schisms in society. Such an unmet need can be hijacked by religious zealots, dangerous national projects – or strange new identity politics on campus. Someone who can't get their kicks through rock music might just go for opioids or cocaine. And, it seems, in the USA today, they are.

Tribalism is built into us through a long evolutionary process and it won't be easy to manage, as studies from the world of psychology have shown. In one experiment, images of people from a different race from the study participants were flashed on a screen for three percent of a second – so fast that the participants were not consciously aware of what they were seeing.

Strong spikes occurred in the activity in the amygdala, the organ in the brain concerned with threat. To some degree, we are wired for to mark the presence of a stranger. However, Will Cunningham at the University of Toronto found that, "When the faces were left on the screen for half a second (a long stretch of time for the brain), the amygdala response was greatly reduced; the prefrontal response was greatly increased, and the more activity recorded in prefrontal cortex, the greater the reduction in the amygdala response."[16] The prefrontal cortex lets us think and judge more rationally and calmly.

Interestingly, the study above found that, if the faces flashed up were those of people from another race whom participants were familiar with or admired, then there was no correlation between amygdala activity and racism scores. "Cultural values and individual experience can overcome the brain's racism... *Familiarity* with 'the other guy' is the most natural defence against blind suspicion," and this takes time.[17]

The answer may lie there. If we take the time to focus without too much emotion, we can get a different view. Thus, though wired to make a difference between 'us' and 'them', we also have the built-in mechanisms to bring in another view, given enough time and exposure, (which, for example, Ms. Merkel did not provide).

This is illustrated in an ancient tale called Time and Pomegranates:

A disciple went to the house of a Sufi physician and asked to become an apprentice in the art of medicine. "You are impatient," said the doctor, "and so you will fail to observe things which you will need to learn." But the young man pleaded and the Sufi agreed to accept him.

After some years the youth felt that he could exercise some of the skills that he had learned. One day a man was walking towards the house and the doctor looking at him from a distance said, "That man is ill, he needs pomegranates."

"You have made the diagnosis let me prescribe for him and I will have done half the work," said the student. "Very well," said the teacher, "providing that you remember that action should also be looked at as illustration." As soon as the patient arrived at the doorstep the student brought him in and said, "You are ill, take pomegranates."

"Pomegranates!!!," shouted the patient, "Pomegranates to you! Nonsense!!!" And he went away. The young man asked his master what the meaning of the interchange had been. "I will illustrate it the next time we get a similar case," said the Sufi.

Shortly afterwards the two were sitting outside the house when the master looked up briefly and saw a man approaching. "Here's an illustration for you: a man who needs pomegranates," he said.

The patient was brought in and the doctor said to him, "Ahh yes... you are a difficult and intricate case I can see that. Mmm... let me see. Yes, you need a special diet. This must be composed of something round, small sacs in it, naturally occurring. An orange – no that would be the wrong colour. Lemons – they're too acid. I HAVE IT !!! Pomegranates." The patient went away delighted and grateful.

"But master,"" said the student, "why did you not say pomegranates straight away?"

"Because," said the Sufi, "he needed time as well as pomegranates.[18]

Indeed, the very awareness that time needs to be managed politically, is not built-in to our decision-making processes. Instead, the political and public space is driven by the hyper media, and the increasingly fast machines at our fingertips.

Mastering the group's political ego, including its drive to supremacy, is a slow and patient process, not a question of rapid response. We have a long way to go to become realistic about 'time' and politics. (But that is the subject of another book...)

Globalization has brought us together, but our psyches remain far apart, we may need to control inflow and an absorption of newcomers in order to give time for adjustment, 'get to know the other guy or gal', and overcome our instinctive reactions. We can't leap to justice and rights and 'Imagine', or hanker to build institutions when the people that fill and use them remain greedy and blind. We may need a long transition period.

In that time, we can pursue a critical process of education and, if our group ego 'dissolves' somewhat, we may find that relations between nations and ethnicities may be far from the hell that has defined human history.

Identity is critical for us; it provides security and a sense of contentment that cannot be wished away. It is also a key means of living out our political ego, and, so, a delicate balance is needed. We may be at that crossroads, which may mean neither leaping towards an abstracted cosmopolitanism, nor remaining in the vicissitudes of identity. Tribalism put into perspective may mean a destiny where our various groups interact more smoothly, and with less volatility. Such a step is beyond taming the ego, it is transforming it. Finally, that Commanding Self can serve.

Once, as I boarded an Air Canada flight to Tel Aviv in Toronto, I saw a young, veiled Muslim woman ahead of me make her way to her seat which, it turned out, was next to that of an old Hasidic Jewish man. They both looked at each other in shock, like deer in the headlights, trying to comprehend that they would have to sit beside each other, and contravene religious protocol, sexual mores and political differences all at once.

But, in an instant, the old man politely invited her to take her seat beside him, and she smiled, and did so. There are some positive effects of globalization. They may still remember that trip together to this day, a hint that humanity and cooperation lives on in all of us.

As Imad Younis, an Israeli and a Palestinian, said: "One state or two states? Who cares? ...What matters is human dignity and equality under the same law. Palestinian kids want to live as well. That's what they want": [19]

Mutual needs satisfaction.

PART VII

A LARGER PURPOSE

THE SPECIAL HUMAN GIVEN: *MEANING*

If you lose any sense of being part of something bigger, then why should you care about your fellow-man?

– James Mattis, former U.S. Marine Corps general and Secretary of Defense[1]

I GREW UP in the suburbs of Toronto, a wonderful place called Don Mills, one of the first 'planned communities' in the world. We had a good life in Canada but, once I began doing summer jobs in my teens, I began to feel a sense of alienation sink in. My instincts told me that the economic machine I was entering would overwhelm the pursuit of greater purpose or dissolve it in a sea of material gain and comfort. I sensed that I was going to become a slave of the system. I joined a punk band to rebel (my version of youthful extremism) but, fortunately or not, my band, The Agitators, was quite useless. So I continued on to university and a somewhat more mainstream life. And I did end up buying a BMW.

Modern society, marked by the accumulation of material objects and instant stimulation, can be high on social alienation and bereft of purpose. American Secretary of Defence, James

Mattis homed right in on it when he described the problems that American veterans faced when they returned home: "They think it's PTSD—which it can be—but it's really about alienation. If you lose any sense of being part of something bigger, then why should you care about your fellow-man?"[2]

Throughout the Middle East, I saw young men living in grey, often ugly, and chaotic suburbs spreading miles and miles around ancient cities. If they do find a job, it's likely to be mechanical, mechanized and boring, and even those are increasingly carried out by robots.[3] We had seen earlier how excited young people will latch on to a variety of ideologies, including dangerous ones, in the search for meaning.

The real threat lies in the lethargy and boredom of modern life. Look at the buildings in the banlieues of Paris, or the crowded, urban outgrowths around cities such as Baghdad, Cairo and Beirut. There might be a modicum of material comfort but not a shred of a link to an organic and living culture, nor certainly any aesthetic beauty.[4][5]

It is not only the violent ideologues that are in spiritual hunger at the banquet of life. Without purpose, the great majority of people may not become an extremist nor violent, but many will go on shopping sprees, pornographic splurges, alcoholic binges, or have social media addictions. I even wonder whether this boredom and lack of meaning does not impel many to support high-minded crusades, or join street demonstrations because the action involved fills that void of meaning. As long as time and effort is spent in the pursuit of material gain, an endless pit of greed, our hunger for something deeper in life remains unattended to.

And so, we can become extreme in a different way, destroying normal relations in favour of a short lived 'high.' This all points to that special human given: meaning. This most powerful of motives can be directed towards more positive efforts, and if properly managed, may surprise as a tool for achieving a fulfilling life.

It may even be that, beyond survival and the shenanigans of the ego, we have a larger purpose, a place to go to that merits some attention.

A LARGER PURPOSE

You really cannot unify all different creeds. But you can disunify what lies behind all of them.

– Idries Shah, *Observations* [1]

ON A CRISP day in Jerusalem, on the Haram Al Sharif/Temple Mount, one has a profound sense of beauty. On that plaza stand the Dome of the Rock, the Al Aqsa Mosque, and the small, unobtrusive Dome of Al Khidr. The site is also one of the most contentious half-acres on the planet, the 'radioactive core' of the Israeli–Palestinian conflict and, ultimately, possibly a Jewish-Muslim conflict. The only reason such a place would be the centre of a fight is that both sides treat it like a political football, rather than a place of worship. They wish to possess and control it.

It is difficult to talk about the Middle East without referring to the role of religion in politics. In varying forms, Judaism, Islam and Christianity become part and parcel of the volatile politics. The culture of the region has turned religion, a potentially positive endeavour, into the claims of one people over another. Maybe it has always been so.

As the examination of cults suggests, part of the purpose of religion is to make sure our groups are coherent, united and strong and facing a common direction, including, importantly, that of defeating an enemy.

Turbocharging identity with religion works. It is used for political purpose because it is *effective*. The success of Iran and Israel in the Middle East today is partly down to the right dose of heritage and religion as a motivating force. Fighting for a tribe or nation is good; fighting for religion is better, but fighting for a tribe or nation in God's name is best. It is the reason that ISIS and their ilk resort to it.

Religion is a powerful tool of social cohesion that has served in the Middle East to merge bickering tribes, whether the 12 Tribes of Israel or, once upon a time, the 12 x 12 tribes of Arabia. But then something else, and more dangerous, takes over.

Middle Eastern religious traditions often express a *preferential* relationship with the divine. For the Jews, it is the sense of being a 'chosen people,' the ones who have a covenant with God, while others do not. For Christians, faith is achieved through the Christ-God as the only road to salvation. For the Muslims, it is the idea that Mohammed is the Final Prophet, with the Koran, the literal Word of God superseding prior revelation.[2] They may all say that they worship the same god, but their actions belie that, and suggest that *their* way is somehow better.

Once believers begin to think that they belong to a unique revelation with a special status, the next step is to believe that one's self, nation and history is unique and superior, the saviour of humanity – by force if necessary. It is that sense of being special and supreme that makes religion a tool for tribal competition and the devaluation of others – a cult indeed.

However, some part of us can go beyond this. A bird's eye view can help us see that we are linked and share something universal, beyond all the tribal battles: "A new study has found people are more likely to value the lives of believers and non-believers equally, if they take the perspective of God. ... The results...suggest a belief in God encourages more equal valuation of human life regardless of religious identity, encouraging application of universal moral rules to believers and nonbelievers alike.... Rather than encouraging divisive tribalism, participants believed that God had relatively stronger preferences than they did to treat the value of human lives equally, regardless of religious identity." [3]

God would likely support mutual needs satisfaction. And this relates back to Israel and Palestine. The experts found "that Muslim Palestinian participants valued Palestinian over Jewish Israeli lives when making difficult moral choices, but believed Allah preferred them to make moral decisions that valued the lives of Palestinians and Jewish Israelis more equally."[4]

It is possible to have more of that 'God perspective' if we lower emotional states enough and permit our minds to tap into larger and finer patterns of life.

Since childhood, I would read about the faiths and notice degrees of commonality, how they represented varied expressions made at different times, and in varying places, of a single shared goal: to reach a greater truth. They were different perspectives on one multi-faceted, changing, and glittering orb. Shams of Tabriz, Rumi's teacher and friend, said that we think God sees us from above, like an authority figure in a cult, whereas he sees from the inside – where the work is. I sensed intuitively that he was right, and that the faiths that had made this region so famous – Islam, Christianity and Judaism and also Zoroastrianism and, in interesting ways, the Yazidi, Bahai and so many others – had all ultimately missed the boat. After the initial, powerful kindling, they got lost. As the quote says at the beginning of this section: "You cannot really unify all different creeds. But you can disunify what lies behind all of them." They had done just that: become 'disunified' by transforming into institutional mechanisms or cults for the pursuit of supremacy by groups or individuals.

Although it may not be possible to unify all creeds, a common understanding can grow about what really lies behind them, and so encourage a return to the origins, to a unity. This understanding, which in a sense never left me, helped give me meaning on my journey.

In January 2015, in the middle of a cold Canadian winter, I took a train from Montreal to Toronto. In the seat beside me was a young man from India who, I soon learned, was studying computer science at a Canadian university. He was reading a book called *Man's Search for Meaning* by Victor Frankl. I had just used a quote from an article about Frankl in a chapter I was writing for this very book, and the coincidence set off an interesting conversation – at the end of which the young man from Kerala gave me his copy (I suppose, convinced by our talk that I would find it valuable).

Victor Frankl was imprisoned by the Nazis for being a Jew. He survived the death camps but, as one might expect, he also suffered enormously. Facing the daily threat of death, he was emaciated, had to shave his face with broken glass, and slept beside victims of typhoid. Shoes were shoddy or unavailable, yet he desperately had to try to avoid blistering his feet, because inmates who could not work were put to death.

Frankl, formerly a psychotherapist, observed himself and other inmates in this horrible experience, and he noted that those who created meaning for themselves in the midst of the terrible suffering – who thought about their wives, or a book they wanted to write, or anything else that mattered in their life

– had a much better chance of survival. Those who gave up on life and its meaning were the first to go. Interestingly, one indicator of trouble was when an inmate started smoking. Giving in to the indulgence meant that the discipline to remain focused on what counted had begun to dissipate.

Frankl serves as a powerful counterpoint to ISIS and other extreme political groups. Terrorists use their misdirected search for meaning, and elevations of holiness, to inflict horror on the planet. And, as such, they are not much different from the Nazis who made Frankl suffer. He, on the other hand, managed to eke meaning out of the very conditions that these malevolent characters inflicted upon him.

Like many extremists, ISIS and the Nazis were trying to change the world to fit an image in their mind, and stop at no end to do so. Frankl knew that all he could change was *himself*. "It is not freedom from conditions, it is freedom to take a stand within conditions, that matters," he writes. He also described 'meaning' as "the last of the human freedoms – to choose one's attitude in *any* given set of circumstances, to choose one's own way."[5] Frankl may have been an exception but he had the bravery to accept reality as it was even under the worst conditions, and still produce something positive. His ability to do so arose out of strength of character, or, a well-developed inner self. Virtuous individuals, like Frankl, who took the right way home, have existed throughout time, heralds of what we all can be.

Meaning, in balance with meeting our other needs, can help us move beyond ourselves, and satisfy us in ways that go beyond feeding a hunger. It is the vector that impels us upwards, away from our ego. As I understand it, true meaning comes through being stretched in what we do and how we think, through service to others, learning new skills or being connected to ideas or philosophies bigger than ourselves so that our lives feel purposeful and even suffering becomes tolerable.

The difference between the extremist's search for God and the real search for meaning lies in how much the search is about meeting one's own needs, and how much it is about serving something or someone else; the extremist's agenda is very well woven into his or her untamed ego.

A sincere search for meaning can slowly grow, like a series of ever-widening concentric circles, to encompass greater connection to the world and its service. Politically, that can mean moving from a sense of 'I', to community or tribe, to nation, to culture to humanity as a whole, each attended to as needed (and only as needed). Certainly, almost every case of trouble and conflict I had encountered in the Middle East could have been mitigated by a greater understanding of the role of meaning in their endeavour.

Unlike today's sad manifestations, the pursuit of that real and profound ground of meaning may be what all the religions of the Middle East were originally about. All of them had once situated the human mission in a much grander scheme than the mere pursuit of self-interest, but they were corrupted by time and greed. They lost *their* purpose, as we are looking for ours.

Today, for those trapped in religions that mimic tribes, nations that encourage supremacy, or an all-consuming economic and techno-mania, such a pursuit of greater meaning may seem like fantasy or an illusion. The ability to perceive that we **are** part of a grand drama, a great play, a story, and that our role is purposeful in this universe may however change our perspective, behaviour and priorities.

This shift may indeed be essential for our survival today because the old systems have led to a cacophony of conflict. The fading away of old faiths, or their fossilized final exposition, may mean that we will develop new ways of understanding what people call 'God,' based on the knowledge of who we truly are.[6]

A former Egyptian Muslim Brother, Abdul Monem Abul Futuh, suggests that "the moral individual, who can distinguish between right and wrong and derives his/her judgments from free will, constitutes the core of Islam."[7] It's that true autonomy that makes us 'religious' in the deepest sense of the word. And it is that freedom, at least politically, that the ideas in this book can help further in developing.

One thing I did learn through my journey through the Middle East is that the toughness of Jibril, the madness of ISIS, and the soft wispy dreams of Puff the Magic Dragon won't get us there. The chaos in Cairo or the cold inhumanity at Erez checkpoint, the legless handicapped victims of the wars in Gaza or Hama are not written in the stars. The answer is not in the Temple Mount, the Haram Al Sharif, or the tomb of a saint or Sufi, nor in the terrible checkpoints between the hills of the West Bank, and the sad and criss-crossed borders of the region.

At some point, the people of the Middle East will cease to dwell on the past that draws mischief on, and the Dog River Tablets will sink into the sea. There is an exit to a more pleasant land where supremacies and exclusivities will go the way of the dodo. There is another way.

The answer is all around us, and, like any good secret, it whispers not shouts. When we master this great paradox within us, that we are both tribal and yet striving for individual independence, that we need to belong and be separate at the same time, and that we are capable of doing so, then, I believe, we can begin to see a more common humanity. It is then that we can begin to see 'the stranger that does not belong' in another light.

If we can begin to be aware of the pitfalls of our natural state, we can develop the kind of mental immunization to our excesses that can start us on an opposite process: one of broadening connection to others and understanding our own and others' emotional needs.

Surely it is this understanding that will finally open Jerusalem's Golden Gate. As Arthur Deikman succinctly put it, another reality may then appear: "There is no them; there is only us."

NOTES

Preface: The Golden Gate

1. Ovid, *Metamorphoses*. London: Penguin Books, 2004.
2. Shams of Tabriz, the Persian poet Rumi's friend and spiritual mentor.

Epigraph

1. Dag Hammarskjold, *Markings*, Translated by Leif Sjoberg and W.H. Auden, Alfred A. Knopf, 2003, p. 82.

Epigraph

1. Arthur Deikman, *Them and Us:, Cult Thinking and the Terrorist Threat.*, Arthur Deikman, Berkeley: Bay Tree Publishing, Berkeley CA, 2003, p. 181.

The Demon and the Happy Couple

1. Idries Shah, *The Commanding Self.* London: The Octagon Press, 1997, p. 332.

Origins: The Dog River Tablets

1. William Shakespeare, *Completed Works*, edited by Jonathan Bate and Eric Rasmussen. Hampshire: Macmillan Publishers, 2007, (*The Tragedy of Othello*, The Moor of Venice, Act I, Scene III), p. 2097.
2. Lebanon or 'Lubnan' in Arabic is named after the colour white, or *laban*, in the ancient Semitic Canaanite language.
3. Michael Reisman, *The Art of the Possible: Diplomatic Alternatives in the Middle East*. Princeton: Princeton University Press, 1970. p. 4.

"A Storm of Emotions... A Tempest of Caprices"

1. Allenby, the hero of the British victory in the Middle East, had just been fired for his terrible performance in the Battle of Arras, France in 1917.
2. The Balfour Declaration proclaimed the intent of the British government in 1917 to create a national home for the Jewish people in Palestine.
3. Much later, I was to learn that during this turbulent period, some trouble-makers had come to our home demanding protection money. My mother, an ardent Lebanese patriot, told them to go to hell.
4. David Remnick, "The Party Faithful," *The New Yorker* (online), January 21, 2013. https://www.newyorker.com/magazine/2013/01/21/the-party-faithful
5. Ibid.
6. Uzi Benziman, "The Real Reason Israel Annexed East Jerusalem," *Haaretz*, May 25, 2017. https://www.haaretz.com/israel-news/.premium.MAGA-ZINE-the-real-reason-israel-annexed-east-jerusalem-1.5476317
7. Ibid. Benziman goes on to write: "This is not to say that the decision makers were not aware of the fateful consequences of the steps they were taking. They were very conscious of the implications, and apprehensive about the possible impact. But they yielded to the tsunami of enthusiasm that was unleashed by the air force's tremendous military triumph in the first hours of the war, and to a thrust for revenge and a desire to take advantage of the opportunity created by the foolish and infuriating behaviour of Jordan's King Hussein, who had joined the fight despite receiving assurances from Eshkol that if Jordan kept out of the hostilities, Israel would not attack it."

Jibril and Puff the Magic Dragon

1. Abu Rami spent many years in an Israeli prison. As a young man, he placed a grenade in an Israeli bus to protest the occupation of his land in 1967. The explosive did not go off, but it landed him 17 years in jail, where he learned Hebrew masterfully. He also came to see the need to live in peace with the Israelis, as long as there is a fair solution for his people. Israeli prison did not cure Jibril Rajoub of his ways. As soon as he exited, he became again involved in the Palestinian *intifadah,* or revolt, of the late 1980s. The Israeli authorities decided to deal with him decisively by dumping him unceremo-niously in southern Lebanon, the first Palestinian to have that honour. Jibril made his way from Lebanon to Tunis to work with the PLO and Yasser Arafat before returning through the Oslo process to become head of security in the West Bank.
2. If he did listen to music, it was likely to be heavy duty Arabic *tarab,* that trance-inducing art—music that goes on for hours and hours (and hours).

Adventures on a Blue Line

1. Except for the Cohiba cigars, some may think this could be a description of Tel Aviv. The two cities are indeed similar – with Tel Aviv somewhat more 'chill', like marijuana, and Beirut, hyper, like cocaine.
2. The Economist, October 9, 2017, http://www.economist.com/news/middle-east-and-africa/21710934-arabs-make-up-just-5-worlds-population-they-account-about-half
3. Frederika Whitehead, "Water Scarcity in Yemen: The Forgotten Conflict," *The Guardian*, April 2, 2015. https://www.theguardian.com/global-development-professionals-network/2015/apr/02/water-scarcity-yemen-conflict?
4. "The 11 Cities most likely to run out of drinking water – like Cape Town," BBC News, Feb. 11, 2018. https://www.bbc.co.uk/news/world-42982959
5. There is evidence that being in a negative environment and having unpleasant experiences such as air pollution, and overcrowding makes us have harsher judgments in daily life, i.e. your average traffic accident can turn into a violent melee. See Jonathan Haidt's *The Righteous Mind: Why Good People are Divided by Politics and Religion.* London: Penguin Books, 2012, pp. 70-71.

Iraq the Splendiferous

1. Christopher Reuter, "Secret Files Reveal the Structure of Islamic State," *Der Spiegel,* April 14, 2015, http://www.spiegel.de/international/world/islamic-state-files-show-structure-of-islamist-terror-group-a-1029274.html

The Missing Piece

1. Barbara Tuchman, "An Inquiry into the Persistence of Unwisdom in Government," *Esquire*, 1979, p. 25
2. The answers come from places we don't normally look to. Dopamine, the reward-motivating neurochemical, is released when we see information that support our beliefs. So, the more we like what we see, the more we want of it, even if it is completely and utterly wrong. Our minds are also made to learn from uncomfortable truths, but in the battle between that and the dopamine rush, unless we make an effort, the latter often wins.
3. https://dictionary.cambridge.org/dictionary/english/ego
4. Peter Mandelson, "Putin is Risking the engine of Russia's Economy," *Financial Times*, May 21, 2014. http://www.ft.com/intl/cms/s/0/955d0176-e02f-11e3-9534-00144feabdc0.html#axzz32QZJjz9s
5. Robert Kaplan, "The Coming Anarchy," *The Atlantic Monthly*, February 1, 1994, https://www.theatlantic.com/magazine/archive/1994/02/the-coming-anarchy/304670/

6. Ibid.

7. Meron Benvenisti, "The Inevitable Bi-National Regime," in *Haaretz*, January 22nd, 2010. http://www.americantaskforce.org/daily_news_article/2010/01/22/1264136400_13

Epigraph

1. Walter Wink, *Collected Readings*. Minneapolis: Fortress Press, 2013, p. 82.

Foundation Stones

1. Michelle Boorstein, "How neuroscience is offering hope for a more peaceful world," *Washington Post*, March 4, 2015.

2. I have met a few politicians and diplomats who have an instinctive understanding of human motivation and behaviour, but even these talented few don't have an explicit understanding of *why* we act as we do.

3. Joe Griffin and Ivan Tyrrell, Human Givens: *A New Approach to Emotional Health and Clear Thinking*. Chalvington: Human Givens Publishing, 2004.

4. This approach is gaining ground, and is being taught and practised in Britain, Ireland, parts of Holland, France, Australia and most lately in the US, to help bring emotional understanding and clear thinking, leading to wellbeing, not only in helping the mentally ill but into schools, social care, businesses, child care and any other organisation where humans learn, work, love and live together.

The Power of Meeting Needs in Politics

1. Christian Jarrett, "The Psychology of Violent Extremism Digested," *Research Digest*, October 27, 2014. https://digest.bps.org.uk/2014/10/27/the-psychology-of-violent-extremism-digested/

2. Thomas Hegghammer (Ed.), *Jihadi Culture: The Art and Social Practises of Militant Islamists*. Cambridge: Cambridge University Press, 2017, p. 35.

3. Todd G. Buckholz, *The Price of Prosperity*. New York: HarperCollins, 2016, p. 3.

4. Frederik Pleitgen, "Author's Journey Inside ISIS: They're 'more dangerous than people realize,'" CNN, January 4, 2015. https://edition.cnn.com/2014/12/22/world/meast/inside-isis-juergen-todenhoefer

5. "Surrounded by positives, young Somali chose ISIS," Al Arabiya News, April 10, 2016. https://english.alarabiya.net/features/2016/04/10/Surrounded-by-positives-young-Somali-chose-ISIS

6. "20 Somali-American youths brought up in Minnesota have disappeared from their family homes, turning up months later as new recruits for Jihad."

See Alexandra Stein, *Terror, Love, & Brainwashing: Attachment in Cults and Totalitarian Systems*. New York: Routledge, 2017, p. 6. "20 Somali-American youths brought up in Minnesota have disappeared from their family homes, turning up months later as new recruits for Jihad."

7. "ISIS Behind the Mask," CNN Special Report, March, 2017. https://www.cnn.com/interactive/2017/03/europe/isis-behind-the-mask/

8. Jarrett, "The Psychology of Violent Extremism – Digested"

9. Interestingly, some more radical right-wingers in the USA may have a similar background: "History will record a preponderance of today's right-wing leaders who emerged in the toniest quarters of the nation's bluest states." See Wil S. Hylton, "Down the Breitbart Hole," *New York Times*, August 16, 2017. https://www.nytimes.com/2017/08/16/magazine/breit-bart-alt-right-steve-bannon.html?

10. http://www.vocativ.com/news/251306/psychology-terrorist/

11. Jarrett, "The Psychology of Violent Extremism – Digested"

12. "In Pictures: The Poppies at the Tower of London," BBC News, November 7, 2014, https://www.bbc.co.uk/news/in-pictures-29935592

13. Tim Wu, *The Attention Merchants*, London: Atlantic Books, 2017, p. 41.

14. "In 2006 Edwin Bakker published a review of hundreds of jihadi terrorists in Europe based on media and court reports. Of the 242 people Bakker identified, most were in their late teens or twenties, and just five were women." Jarrett, "The Psychology of Violent Extremism – Digested"

15. Joe Herbert, "What every dictator knows: young men are natural fanatics," *Aeon*, February 1, 2016. https://aeon.co/ideas/what-every-dictator-knows-young-men-are-natural-fanatics

16. Olivier Roy, "Le djihadisme est une révolte générationnelle et nihiliste," *Le Monde*, Nov. 23, 2015. http://www.lemonde.fr/idees/article/2015/11/24/le-djihadisme-une-revolte-generationnelle-et-nihiliste_4815992_3232.html

17. Joshua Holland, "Here's what a man who studied every suicide attack in the world says about ISIS," *The Nation*, December 2, 2015. https://www.thenation.com/article/heres-what-a-man-who-studied-every-suicide-attack-in-the-world-says-about-isiss-motives/

18. Jonathan Haidt, *The Righteous Mind*, p. 13-14.

The Tragic Brilliance of ISIS

1. "Anthropologist seeks the roots of terrorism," *Scientific American*, January 20, 2015. http://www.scientificamerican.com/article/anthropologist-seeks-the-roots-of-terrorism/

2. "ISIS Behind the Mask," CNN Special Report

3. Ibid

4. Joe Herbert, "What every dictator knows: young men are natural fanatics"

5. Jarrett, "The Psychology of Violent Extremism – Digested"

6. ISIS and other violent radical groups did not only meet needs, they used cultural material to do it, devising apparently beautiful realms and high

ideals. The jihadis develop a comprehensive culture for young people to be immersed in. They lure people in with dreams while their opponents in governments drown in technocratic and bureaucratic jargon.

7. Hegghammer, p. 33.
8. Hegghammer, p. 150.

"Na ba zar, na ba zor, na ba zahr"

1. Before the Israeli occupation, Jerusalem had a Muslim mayor and a Christian deputy mayor to provide some balance between the communities.
2. The same may be said of the Kurds.
3. Seyed Hossein Mousavian and Mohammad Ali Shabani, "How to Talk to Iran," in *New York Times*, January 3, 2013. https://www.nytimes.com/2013/01/04/opinion/how-to-talk-to-iran.html
4. Ibid.
5. "Understanding Iran," Al Bab: Impressions of the Middle East, Past & Present, April 16, 2009. http://albabblog.blogspot.com.es/2009/04/understanding-iran.html
6. Thomas Edbrink and David E. Sanger, "US Increases Pressure of Economic War on Tehran," *New York Times*, February 7, 2013.https://www.nytimes.com/2013/02/07/world/middleeast/us-ratchets-up-an-economic-war-against-tehran.html
7. Mousavian and Shibani, "How to Talk to Iran"
8. The role of another often ignored basic human need, attention, is also important here. People panic if they don't get the right amount of attention. "If our need for attention is not met ... we become attention seekers, which can become destructive to relationships. Any healthy human need, if unnurtured, can swell into a destructive want," say Griffin and Tyrrell. In many ways, Iran had been seeking American attention through direct talks, but also through wild and aggressive actions and words designed to attract attention – whatever works.
9. For his part, Donald Trump was trying to redress this, if in a possibly destructive fashion, by withdrawing from the nuclear deal in 2018 and confronting Iran, (*how* we pursue our needs is as important as identifying them).

Death By Identity

1. Sergei Guriev, "In Russia, it's not the Economy, Stupid," *New York Times*, December 25, 2016 http://www.nytimes.com/2016/12/25/opinion/in-russia-its-not-the-economy-stupid.html?
2. Vladimir Putin adopted this philosophy of *passionarnost* or 'passionarity.' "Putin's definition of passionarity (from the Latin word *passio*, 'moving

forward and embracing change') .... would be something like 'capacity for suffering.' It was a word with allusions to the New Testament and the crucifixion that had been dreamt up by Gumilev during his 14 years in Siberian prison camps." A sense of common purpose and a capacity of suffering are powerful forces. See Charles Clover, "Lev Gumilev: Passion, Putin and Power," *Financial Times*, March 11, 2016. http://www.ft.com/cms/s/2/ede1e5c6-e0c5-11e5-8d9b-e88a2a889797.html.

3. https://en.wikipedia.org/wiki/Ibn_Khaldun.

4. His view is echoed by Amar, a commander among the Syrian opposition, "We started the revolution because we wanted to be treated like humans, we are looking of our humanity. All my life I have been treated like an inferior, a human being of the 10th class, while Assad and his people controlled the country. We also have a right in this country." Gaith Abdul Ahad, "Inside Syria: The Rebel Call for Arms and Ammunition," *The Guardian*, 11 December 2011. https://www.theguardian.com/world/2011/dec/11/inside-syria-rebels-call-arms

Identity Matters

1. Frederick Starr, *Lost Enlightenment: Central Asia's Golden Age From the Arab Conquest to Tamerlane*. Princeton: Princeton University Press, p. 532.

2. https://en.wikipedia.org/wiki/Shibboleth

3. Dr. Erol Katiricioglu, "Political and Economic Trends 2002-2017: Implications for Conflict Resolution in Turkey," Democratic Progress Institute, London, Nov. 2017. https://www.democraticprogress.org/wp-content/uploads/2017/11/Political-and-Economic-Trends-2002-to-2017.pdf

The Hive Switch

1. Haidt, *The Righteous Mind*, p. 313.

2. It turns out that only 5% of any crowd is needed to move in a direction for the whole group to move like a herd. The other 95% follow without awareness. Rick Nauert, "Herd Mentality Explained," *Psych Central*, May 3, 2019. https://psychcentral.com/news/2017/02/15/herd-mentality-explained/1922.html

3. Robert Ardrey, *The Territorial Imperative*. New York: Atheneum, 1966, p. 171.

4. David McMillan, "Exposing the righteous mind: An interview with Jonathan Haidt," *Thought Catalog*, March 21, 2012. https://thoughtcatalog.com/david-mcmillan/2012/03/exposing-the-righteous-mind-an-interview-with-jonathan-haidt/

5. Haidt, *The Righteous Mind*, p. 282.

'Cult u re': The Cult in Culture

1. Jason Elliot, *The Madhouse*, Beauxdraps Publishing, UK, 2019, p. 5.
2. Eran Tzidkiyahu, "The Israelis Who Take Rebuilding the Third Temple Very Seriously," *Haaretz*, August 10, 2017. http://www.haaretz.com/israel-news/.premium-1.805977
3. Amir Oren, "They were not confused by the facts," *Haaretz*, September 27, 2009.
4. Of course, it is certainly not just the Middle East that suffers from this. It is a pervasive human condition. During the Vietnam War, Secretary of Defence Robert McNamara used marvellous statistical and analytical techniques to help America win the war, yet it only sank more deeply into the morass. And, American decision makers ignored data to invade Iraq in 2003, accepting only the information required to justify their pre-cooked decision; again, a state of diminished realism.
5. 'Tribes With Flags' is part of a phrase attributed to Tahseen Bashir, an Egyptian diplomat (April 1925-June 11, 2002). Regarding his belief in the centrality of Egypt within the Middle East he opined: "Egypt is the only nation-state in the Arab world; the rest are just tribes with flags." https://en.wikipedia.org/wiki/Tribes_with_Flags
6. His work is summed up in the posthumous compilation, *Meditations on a Blue Vase*. See https://www.deikman.com.
7. Karen Armstrong, "The Myth of Religious Violence," *The Guardian*, September 25, 2014. http://www.theguardian.com/world/2014/sep/25/-sp-karen-armstrong-religious-violence-myth-secular
8. Ghaith Abdul Ahad, "After the Liberation of Mosul, an Orgy of Killing," *The Guardian*, November 21, 2017. https://www.theguardian.com/world/2017/nov/21/after-the-liberation-of-mosul-an-orgy-of-killing?
9. Robert F. Worth, "The Pillars of Arab Despotism," *New York Review of Books*, Nov. 9, 2014. https://www.nybooks.com/articles/2014/10/09/pillars-arab-despotism/
10. Ashraf El-Sherif, "The Muslim Brotherhood's Failures," Carnegie Endowment for International Peace, July 1, 2014. http://carnegieendowment.org/2014/07/01/egyptian-muslim-brotherhood-s-failure/
11. https://russiancouncil.ru/en/analytics-and-comments/analytics/pereosmyslivaya-pereosmyslenie/
12. Matthew Syed, *Rebel Ideas: The Power of Diverse Thinking. London:* John Murray, 2019, p. 91.
13. Former Israeli official in a private conversation.

The Stars in Jerusalem – Cult Central

1. Arthur Deikman, p. 114.
2. This can even happen from a considerable distance. The Waco disaster of 1993 was impelled by a revelation about Jerusalem by David Koresh. See Nettanel Slyomovics, "Waco Started With a Divine Revelation in Jerusalem. It Ended With 76 Dying in a Fire on Live TV," in *Haaretz*, February 2, 2018. https://www.haaretz.com/us-news/.premium.MAGAZINE-waco-the-jerusalem-revelation-that-ended-with-76-dying-in-a-fire-1.5846185
3. Queen Helen Street in 'West Jerusalem' in the Musrara area, once a Muslim district that was taken over by Zionists in the fighting of 1948. I lived in a late 19th century stone home that was typical for the Muslim middle class that left the Old City for more space and leisure in that period. The house was spacious with half-meter thick walls that warmed the house in winter and cooled it in summer. The neighbourhood still had the plaque of an Arab dentist at the entrance to one of the houses and some of the outside walls were pockmarked by the fighting that took place between east and west sides of the city, especially in the period 1948-1967 when Jordanian troops in control of East Jerusalem would still shoot at the West side.
4. Recently, the neighbouring Negev desert was used for training for trips to Mars because of its similarity to the planet's landscape.
5. Al Aqsa refers to the 'furthest mosque' that was built in Jerusalem on the site of the Prophet Mohammad's night journey to heaven. This mosque was built on the southern corner of the esplanade also known as the Temple Mount where, it is believed, the Jewish temple once stood. It would have been natural for early Muslims, who partly derived their faith out of the monotheism of Judaism to some degree, to create a link to such a site. A later shrine was built in the middle of the esplanade, the Dome of the Rock, on the site of the rock that is believed to be where Abraham was ready to sacrifice his son.
6. Peter Frankopan, *The Silk Roads*. London: Bloomsbury, 2015, p. 95.
7. Karen Armstrong, *Jerusalem: One City, Three Faiths*. New York: Alfred A. Knopf, 1996, p. 25.
8. One memorable exception is Omar Ibn El Khattab, the Muslim conqueror of the city who refused to pray in the Church of the Holy Sepulchre for fear that it would then be turned into a mosque. He went some 50 yards away to pray, and now a mosque stands there in commemoration of his decision and prayer.
9. Karen Armstrong, "The Myth of Religious Violence," *The Guardian*, September 25, 2014. https://www.theguardian.com/world/2014/sep/25/-sp-karen-armstrong-religious-violence-myth-secular
10. Dominic Johnson, *God is Watching You*. New York: Oxford University Press, pp. 174-175.

Epigraph

1. William Shakespeare, *Completed Works*, edited by Jonathan Bate and Eric Rasmussen. Hampshire: Macmillan Publishers, 2007, (*The Tragedy of Julius Caesar*, Act I, Scene II), p. 1810.

The Manipulator's Art

1. Ardrey, p. 237.
2. Bergen Evans, *The Natural History of Nonsense*. New York: Vintage Books, p. 262.
3. The Israelis were convinced by the amount of blood spilled at the site that the soldiers had been killed during the operation, and they asked the UN to stop the talks. They turned out to be right.
4. This may have been fuelled, or perhaps exacerbated, by the death of his son in the fight against the Israeli occupation of southern Lebanon.
5. By 2021, Hizballah's status in Lebanon had slipped considerably. Their involvement in supporting corrupt politicians, handicapping the Lebanese economy, and their possible involvement in the port explosion woke Lebanese citizens up to the problem.
6. Robert Forsyth Worth, "Hezbollah Seeks to Marshall the Piety of the Young," in *New York Times*, November 21, 2008. http://www.nytimes.com/2008/11/21/world/middleeast/21lebanon.html
7. David Brooks, "The Anti-Party Men: Trump, Carson, Sanders," *New York Times*, September 8, 2015. http://www.nytimes.com/2015/09/08/opinion/the-anti-party-men-trump-carson-sanders-and-corbyn.html?
8. "Wang Qishan, puissant vice-president chinois," *Le Monde*, March 19 2018.
9. David Gardner, "Turkey: Spinning into the Vortex?" *Financial Times*, January 9, 2015. https://www.ft.com/content/cdc5c064-96c0-11e4-922f-00144feabdc0
10. Ahmet Hakan, "Why is he doing this?", *Hurriyet Daily News*, November 9, 2013, https://www.hurriyetdailynews.com/why-is-he-doing-this--57617
11. See "The Cult of the Leader, in Al Bab Blog. http://albabblog.blogspot.com.es/2013/10/the-cult-of-leader.html
12. Identified in the human givens approach as our means to help meet our needs.
13. Ivan Tyrrell and John Bell, "Donald Trump, Demagoguery & Attractive Illusions, " Al Jazeera (online), May 12, 2016. https://www.aljazeera.com/indepth/opinion/2016/05/donald-trump-demagoguery-attractive-illusions-160505092138636.html
14. A term coined by Human Givens co-founders Joe Griffin and Ivan Tyrrell to describe the waking form of the REM (rapid eye movement) dream stage of sleep, with which it has clear physiological similarities. See Joe Griffin and Ivan Tyrrell, *Dreaming Reality: how dreaming keeps us sane or can drive us*

mad. East Sussex: HG Publishing, 2004. Revised and reprinted in 2014 under the title, *Why We Dream*.

15. Carlotta Gall, "Sermons and Shouted Insults: How Erdogan Keeps Turkey Spellbound," in *New York Times*, April 2nd, 2018. https://www.nytimes.com/2018/04/02/world/middleeast/erdogan-turkey.html

16. Tim Wu, p.16.

17. Carlotta Gall, "Sermons and Shouted Insults: How Erdogan Keeps Turkey Spellbound"

18. Gary Younge, "What Will Barack Obama's Legacy Be?" *The Guardian*, March 19, 2016. http://www.theguardian.com/us-news/2016/mar/19/yes-tried-barack-obama-legacy-gary-younge

19. Carlotta Gall, "Sermons and Shouted Insults: How Erdogan Keeps Turkey Spellbound."

Trump's World - Our World

1. Idries Shah, *The Way of the Sufi*, London: The Octagon Press, 1980 p. 90.

2. Paul Goble, "Russian Population's Reaction to Skripal Case More Disturbing than a First Glance Suggests, Psychologist Says," *Stop Fake*, March 14, 2018. https://www.stopfake.org/en/russian-population-s-reaction-to-skripal-case-more-disturbing-than-a-first-glance-suggests-psychologist-says/

3. Douglas Jehl, "For Egyptians, Something Sexy to Beat Their Gums About," *New York Times*, July 10, 1996.

4. Dominic Johnson, *God is Watching You: How the Fear of God Makes Us Human*. New York: Oxford University Press, 2015, p. 122.

5. Sean Illing, "Two eminent political scientists: The problem with democracy is voters" in *Vox*, Juen 24, 2017. https://www.vox.com/policy-and-politics/2017/6/1/15515820/donald-trump-democracy-brexit-2016-election-europe

6. http://internationalpoliticaltheory.blogspot.com/2011/11/joseph-schumpeter-on-democracy.html

7. Before he was voted out of office in Canada, former Prime Minister Stephen Harper promoted legislation to prevent terrorism in the country. It was surprisingly sweeping: giving the Canadian Security Intelligence Service powers beyond intelligence gathering (to actively target threats and derail plots); creating new offences (criminalising 'terrorist propaganda' and the 'promotion of terror'); lowering the legal threshold to trigger detention to those who *may* carry out an offence from the existing standard of *will* carry out; and much more. Yet Canadians, in their ignorance, permitted him to pursue his goal. The government did not explain how this new law would prevent terror, but 82 percent of Canadians supported the bill anyway. Why not? Strong support also came from people who only *heard* about the bill but did not know its details. Their instincts and fears had kicked in.

8. Nathalie Wolchover, "People Aren't Smart Enough for Democracy to Flourish, Scientists Say," *Live Science*, February 28, 2012. https://www.livescience.com/18706-people-smart-democracy.html

9. Timothy Egan, "The Dumbed Down Democracy," in *New York Times*, August 26, 2018. http://www.nytimes.com/2016/08/26/opinion/the-dumbed-down-democracy.html?

10. George Saunders, "Who are all these Trump Supporters?" *The New Yorker*, July 4, 2016, http://www.newyorker.com/magazine/2016/07/11/george-saunders-goes-to-trump-rallies

Needs Met Badly: The Road to Destruction

1. Since that time, a Lebanese uprising has begun, based exactly on this premise.

2. "A Look at the Root Causes of the Arab Revolution," *Der Spiegel*, May 20, 2011.http://www.spiegel.de/international/world/rising-literacy-and-a-shrinking-birth-rate-a-look-at-the-root-causes-of-the-arab-revolution-a-763537-2.html

3. In the Middle East, this can also expand into a nexus between state and militias, whether *shabiha* in Syria, *Hashd El Sha'bi* in Iraq or more informal gangs that somehow work for the state, or one state or another. These gangs roam to pick off the gadflies, the dissidents, while the majority of people do not see how the loss of truthtellers will ultimately result in a failed society. We see this pattern in Syria with the Assads, in Lebanon with Hizballah, and, in some ways, in today's Egypt.

4. Thomas Friedman, "Democracy is in Recession," *New York Times*, February 18, 2015. http://www.nytimes.com/2015/02/18/opinion/thomas-friedman-democracy-is-in-recession.html

5. The dates mentioned may be related to the spread of the smartphone. New technology certainly permits us to gain new information – and new friends – but if the mind is shaped around the device's narrowing circuits, our capacity to solve our problems also narrows. We become effectively mentally hobbled.

6. Sarah Chayes, *Thieves of State*. New York: W.W. Norton and Company, 2015, p. 85.

7. Corruption is not just for the wealthy and powerful. Prior to the 2008 economic crash, Americans were buying homes without any money down, or demonstrating income to the banks through tax returns. This may be the fault of those encouraging them, but it is also a demonstration of the eagerness for easy money and riches among the whole population. When corruption is rampant in so many places, when all are seeking the greatest gain in the shortest time, no matter the cost, anything goes.

8. Todd G. Buchholz, *The Price of Prosperity: Why Rich Nations Fail and How to Renew Them*. New York: Harper, 2016 pp. 5, 59.

Like Father, Like Son

1. O.M. Burke, *Among the Dervishes*. London: The Octagon Press, 1973, p. 135
2. A former Egyptian foreign minister confirmed to me that he believed the same thing prior to February 2011: Egypt would not have a revolution.
3. The Mugamaa is a large ugly building in Tahrir Square where anyone who had any paperwork to do with the Egyptian government had to visit to conduct business. It was Soviet in style, Kafkaesque in feel, and an anthill of semi-chaotic activity.
4. Today, Boulaq is ploughed under, with plans to build Dubai-style skyscrapers in its place. That is certainly a function of greater profit seeking on land in central Cairo. But it is also a convenient way to move a potentially troublesome population away from the heart of power. The residents of Boulaq, I understand, have been relocated to one of the new satellite cities around Cairo.
5. "Survey of Economic and Social Developments in the Arab World," United Nations Economic and Social Commission for Western Asia, 2016. https://www.unescwa.org/sites/www.unescwa.org/files/publications/files/survey-economic-social-development-arab-region-2015-2016-english.pdf
6. Stein, p. 26.
7. Burke, p. 135.

Epigraph

1. https://www.goodreads.com/quotes/7363158-the-summary-of-the-advice-of-all-prophets-is-this

The Bottom Line: Ana wa Bas

1. A verse from a classical Arabic poem mentioned to me by a Syrian in a conversation in Brussels. It may be a reference to Al Mutannabi.
2. *Nafs El Amarra* in Arabic.

The Missing Piece - Redux

1. "Isaac Bashevis Singer's Universe", New York Times, December 3, 1978 https://www.nytimes.com/1978/12/03/archives/isaac-bashevis-singers-universe-errors-and-betrayals.html
2. North Vietnamese soldier, Bao Ninh, in *The Vietnam War: A Film by Ken Burns and Lynn Novick*, episode 10.

Making the Human Disappear

1. *The Human Givens Charter*, Chalvington: Human Givens Publishing, 2004. https://www.hgi.org.uk/hg-charter/human-givens-charter

2. Scott Atran and Nafees Hamid, "Paris: The War ISIS Wants," *New York Review*, November 16, 2015. http://www.nybooks.com/daily/2015/11/16/paris-attacks-isis-strategy-chaos/ As necessary as some security responses may be in the immediate term, they have their limits. This is what happened in France after the terror attacks in Paris in November, 2015: "Keeping full track of those suspected of being prone to violent acts is practically impossible: around-the-clock surveillance of a single individual requires 10 to 20 security agents, of which there are only 6500 for all of France. Nor is it a matter of controlling the flow of people into France. France's Centre for the Prevention of Sectarian Drift Related to Islam (CPDSI) estimates that 90 percent of French citizens who have radical Islamist beliefs have French grandparents and 80 percent come from non-religious families. In fact, most Europeans who are drawn into jihad are 'born again' into radical religion by their social peers."

   Only half a decade later, developments in digital technology may facilitate this kind of monitoring; however, I for one will not relish living in a Big Brother world of such surveillance. Jails are also effectively breeding grounds for the problem, not solutions. Egyptian jihadism was born in Egyptian political prisons in the 1960s; ISIS leaders were formed in American jails in Iraq, and, today, French extremists graduate from French prisons. A study conducted by the Rand Corporation has shown that among 268 terrorist groups that operated between 1968 and 2006, only 7 percent were defeated militarily. Even when they were, they later morphed into more virulent forms, often simply shifting locale. Vladimir Putin has said that 5000 to 7000 people from Russia and other former Soviet states are fighting for ISIS in Syria and may one day return to haunt Russia.

3. https://en.wikiquote.org/wiki/Ehud_Barak

4. Kirk Semple, Paulina Villegas and Elisabeth Malkin, "Mexico Earthquake Kills Hundreds, Trapping Many under Rubble," *New York Times*, September 19, 2017. https://www.nytimes.com/2017/09/19/world/americas/mexico-earthquake.html

5. "Arab Conspiracy Theories Surrounding the Tsunami," *Likoed*, Jan. 7, 2005, https://likud.nl/2005/01/arab-conspiracy-theories-surrounding-the-tsunami/

6. Johnson, p. 158.

7. Johnson, p. 198.

8. For a crucial understanding of the difference between how our minds engage with reality and then re-present it, see Iain McGilchrist's, *The Master and his Emissary*. For an amusing look at the proliferation of experts and their vices, see Nassim Nicholas Taleb's, *Skin in the Game*.

9. Ralph Waldo Emerson, "Politics," in American Verse Project, University of Michigan Humanities Text Initiative (HTI), https://quod.lib.umich.e-du/a/amverse/BAD1982.0001.001/1:7.3?rgn=div2;view=fulltext

Mutual Needs Satisfaction

1. Idries Shah, *Reflections*. New York: Penguin Books, 1977, p. 122.
2. The Geneva Accords, an unofficial negotiation by civil society, effectively traded off Israeli sovereignty on the Temple Mount for the Palestinian Right of Return, both important intangible issues and received much criticism from both sides for doing so. Trading sacred values one for the other can inflame rather than resolve.
3. Boaz Hameiri & Arie Nadler, "Looking Backward to Move Forward: Effects of Acknowledgment of Victimhood on Readiness to Compromise for Peace in the Protracted Israeli–Palestinian Conflict," in *Personality and Social Psychology Bulletin*, 2017, 43, 4, pp. 555-69. http://journals.sagepub.-com/doi/abs/10.1177/0146167216689064
4. Bernard Avishai, "A Palestinian Research Centre Comes Under Threat in a Government Crackdown," in *The New Yorker*, February 4, 2018. https://www.newyorker.com/news/daily-comment/a-palestinian-research-center-comes-under-threat-in-a-government-crackdown
5. One of the best examples of how this works was Sadat's visit to Jerusalem as a precedent to his country's talks with Israel. By telling Israelis through a clear and visible act that he was ready to recognize them in the region, he loosened up their capacity to negotiate. As much as this did not help the Palestinians, it did help Egypt to retrieve Sinai.
6. A proposal put forward to Israel by the Arab League in 2002 as a solution to the Arab-Israeli conflict.
7. The Conciliators Guild, https://www.conciliators-guild.org/

Pragmatic and Creative: A More Intelligent Citizen

1. *The Natural History of Nonsense*, p. 262.
2. He also told me that he supported a vote of "non-confidence" in the ballot box, for those who did not want to choose any of the available candidates. He figured if enough people voted for non-confidence, the politicians would have to give up their blather, and meet normal people's needs.
3. Lorena Cotza, "Pakistani Peacebuilder Receives International Recognition," Peace Direct, October 26, 2013, https://www.peacedirect.org/gulalai-international-recognition/
4. I have supported the development of a "Conflict Resolution Olympics," a competition to encourage professionals, publics and youth, to develop

creative solutions for ongoing conflicts, and compete over which is best. We need to become better at preventing political and violent conflict, so why not inject a competitive and audacious spirit to the resolution of global conflicts, encouraging professionals, as well as the public, to employ greater creativity in resolving ongoing conflicts today?

5. Hana Rosin, "How a Danish Town Helped Young Muslims Turn Away from ISIS," in NPR, July 15, 2016, http://www.npr.org/sections/health-shots/2016/07/15/485900076/how-a-danish-town-helped-young-muslims-turn-away-from-isis

6. "The Psychological Benefits of Receiving Real-Life Altruism," Edward Hoffman and Catalina Acosta-Orozco, *Journal of Humanistic Psychology*, 2017, https://doi.org/10.1177%2F0022167817690280.

7. Oliver Burroughs, *Moneyland: Why Thieves and Crooks now Rule the World and How to Take it Back*. London: Profile Books, 2018, p. 17.

8. Do they arrive at power as such, or do they become so once there? "Mercedes drivers were a quarter as likely to stop at a crossing and four times more likely to cut in front of another car than drivers of beaten-up Ford Pintos and Dodge Colts. The more luxurious the vehicle, the more entitled its owner felt to violate the laws of the highway."

9. Matthew Sweet, "Does Power Really Corrupt?", *The Economist: 1843 Magazine*, June-July 2016. https://www.1843magazine.com/features/does-power-really-corrupt

10. Sean Illing, "What Machiavelli can teach us about Trump and the decline of liberal democracy," in *Vox*, July 24, 2017, https://www.vox.com/2017/7/24/15913826/machiavelli-donald-trump-democracy-america-erica-benner

11. As we saw earlier, demagogues have a natural instinct for abusing our nature for their ends. As successful as this may be in helping them gain domestic power, it often fails in seeing that the neighbours can also rally a crowd. On the premise that we are the only driven ones in the great cult silo, we can end up with the invasion of Moscow, where the citizen ends up as nothing but cannon-fodder. Like much bad wine, the demagogue and the clever leader may be good for local consumption, but he does not export well at all. Caveat emptor.

12. Sean Illing, "What Machiavelli can teach us about Trump and the decline of liberal democracy"

Find a Mirror

1. Sayd Bahoddine Majrouh, *Rire Avec Dieu: Aphorismes et Contes Soufis*. Paris: Albin Michel, 1995, p. 183.

2. Ivan Tyrrell, *Listening to Idries Shah: How Understanding Can Grow*, Chalvington: HG Publishing, 2017.

3. Imposing law through more government, soon to be abetted by A.I., is creating a new and larger pen for the blissfully distracted, a form of subtle

control that may have never been seen before in human history. The torture chamber is louder and more dramatic than facial recognition, social credits and political correctness, but they are all forms of coercion.

Making the Human Reappear

1. Hammarskjold, p. 82.
2. Regarding the role of leaders, interestingly, some of Nelson Mandela's closest confidants advised him to turn down the Nobel Peace Prize and not share it with his former oppressors. He chose the road of reconciliation. The quality and courage of leaders, to help their nation deal with vulnerability and move into the future is key. Peter Frankopan, *The New Silk Roads: The Present and Future of the World*. London: Bloomsbury, 2018, p. 18.

Epigraph

1. Idries Shah, *Caravan of Dreams*. London: The Octagon Press, 1995, p. 18.

"He needed time"

1. Giovanna de Garayalde, *Jorge Luis Borges: Sources and Illumination*. London: The Octagon Press, p. 78.
2. William Anderson, *The Face of Glory*. London: Bloomsbury, p. 64-65.
3. Amanda Holpuch, "Muslim woman ejected from Trump Rally after silent protest," *The Guardian*, January 9, 2016. https://www.theguardian.com/us-news/2016/jan/09/muslim-woman-ejected-donald-trump-rally-silent-protest
4. Anne-Sylvaine Chassany and Guy Chazan, "European Politics: Leaders Struggle to Contain Rising Populism," *Financial Times*, December 13, 2017. https://www.ft.com/content/7d012adc-dc32-11e7-a039-c64b1c09b482
5. David Cameron's referendum on Brexit was little more than an attempt to manage those to his right politically – and unexpected consequences resulted.
6. Chassany and Chazan, "European Politics: Leaders Struggle to Contain Rising Populism"
7. Some believe that Germany has managed well so far, and the extremists are being managed. Molly Worthen, "Where in the World Can we Find Hope?" *New York Times*, February 18, 2017. https://www.nytimes.com/2017/02/18/opinion/sunday/where-in-the-world-can-we-find-hope.html.
8. Ross Douthat, "The Crisis For Liberalism," *New York Times*, November 20, 2016. https://www.nytimes.com/2016/11/20/opinion/sunday/the-crisis-for-liberalism.html
9. Charles Clover, "Lev Gumilev: Passion, Putin and Power"

10. Buchholz, p. 144.
11. Ross Douthat, "The Crisis for Liberalism," *New York Times*, November 19, 2016 https://www.nytimes.com/2016/11/20/opinion/sunday/the-crisis-for-liberalism.html
12. Iain McGilchrist, *The Master and his Emissary: The Divided Brain and the Making of the Western World*. London: Yale University Press, 2012, p. 436.
13. Goodhart, p. 21.
14. Ashley J. Tellis, "Are India-Pakistan Talks worth a Damn?" Carnegie Endowment for International Peace, September 20, 2017. http://carnegieendowment.org/2017/09/20/are-india-pakistan-peace-talks-worth-damn-pub-73145
15. Haidt, *The Righteous Mind*, p. 343.
16. Marc Lewis, "Hate Trump Supporters? Hate Liberals? Here's Why," *The Guardian*, February 7, 2017. https://www.theguardian.com/commentisfree/2017/feb/07/trump-liberals-hate-brain-amygdala-neuroscience
17. Ibid.
18. David Ault – Giving voice to the words of Idries Shah, The Idries Shah Foundation, April 15, 2019, https://idriesshahfoundation.org/news/david-ault-giving-voice-to-the-words-of-idries-shah
19. Roger Cohen, "Why Israel Still Refuses to Choose," *New York Times*, October 30, 2016, http://www.nytimes.com/2016/10/30/opinion/sunday/why-israel-still-refuses-to-choose.html

The Special Human Given: Meaning

1. Dexter Filkins, "James Mattis: A Warrior in Washington," *The New Yorker*, May 22, 2017. http://www.newyorker.com/magazine/2017/05/29/james-mattis-a-warrior-in-washington
2. Ibid.
3. I sensed this looking at some of the EU institutional structures in Brussels, which are modern, sleek, but made of cold metal, all somehow inhuman. Surely, they must be affecting the mental states of the bureaucrats inhabiting them. They may not be the breeding ground of extremism, but they may cause depression and anxiety.
4. Some have demonstrated how the image of chaotic urban growth from above looks remarkably like the unchecked growth of cancer cells.
5. Brianna Rennix and Nathan J. Robinson, "Why you hate Contemporary Architecture," *Current Affairs*, October 31, 2017. https://www.currentaffairs.org/2017/10/why-you-hate-contemporary-architecture

A Larger Purpose

1. Idries Shah, *Observations*, London: ISF Publishing, 2019, p. 113.

2. The relationship between being an Arab and a Muslim is a special one because it was the Arabs who embraced and spread Islam throughout the world – and the Koran is written in Arabic, considered a holy language.

3. Sarah Griffiths, "Jesus saves! Belief in God encourages people to value the lives of others equally even those from other religions," *Daily Mail,* Dec. 29, 2015. http://www.dailymail.co.uk/sciencetech/article-3377467/Jesus-saves-Belief-God-encourages-people-value-lives-equally-religions.html

4. Sarah Griffiths, ibid.

5. Emily Esfahani Smith, "A Psychiatrist Who Survived The Holocaust Explains Why Meaningfulness Matters More Than Happiness," *Business Insider,* October 22, 2014. http://www.businessinsider.com/a-lesson-about-happiness-from-a-holocaust-survivor-2014-10

6. As the Oracle of Delphi predicted so many years ago, "Know thyself, and you are going to know the gods." In so many ways there is nothing new under the sun, and the ancient Greeks had a lot of things right.

7. Nathan Brown, Amr Hamzawy, "Islamist Movements and the Democratic Process in the Arab World: Exploring the Gray Zones," Carnegie Papers, Middle East Series, no. 67, 2006.

ACKNOWLEDGEMENTS

My deepest thanks for those who have accompanied, advised, prodded, commented, read, poked, and always demanded better during the writing of this book. Above all, Ivan Tyrrell and John Zada, friends and colleagues who through their advice and regular discussions are, effectively, co-writers. But also, Denise Winn, Arlene Blackwell, Julia Welstead, Julie Issa, Celia Carina Clinciu, Christine Merjanian, Fady Atallah, Karim Al Rawi, Silva Kanterava, Goldie Schermann, Emilie La Cour, and Charlotte Mounier for their input and contribution, and, the island of Crete for its inspiring vistas, raki-filled mornings and welcoming people. Last but far from least, my brother Michael, whose comments were invaluable, and who still demands that I change the title.

For those interested in the ideas in this book and how they are being disseminated and worked on politically, please visit the website of The Conciliators Guild:

www.conciliators-guild.org

Index

Q

R

Conciliators Guild

The Conciliators Guild Principles

The prime purpose of politics is to help people and societies flourish productively in peace.

At a time of increased political turbulence and social unravelling, *The Conciliators Guild* aims to help diminish political polarization and conflict. There is a critical need to balance narrow political interests with broader perspectives. More flexible and creative minds are required to attend to today's complexities.

The Guild disseminates knowledge that nurtures multi-perspective approaches and the pursuit of "mutual needs satisfaction" for all concerned. It pursues this through courses, practical projects, events centred around key ideas, and, above all, an international network of like-minded individuals who support this mature approach.

The Guild's Principles

Guild members commit to the development of greater excellence and less polarization in politics by working to uphold the following principles:

1. **Context is everything.** The prime purpose of politics and policymaking is the improvement of human wellbeing, both physical *and* emotional. This necessitates the consideration of as many concerned parties and influencing factors as possible, thus expanding context. Although politics are often depicted as the pursuit of power and singular agendas, or defined by opportunistic decisions, it is the consequences of political actions on individuals and societies that matter.

2. **Risk is an unavoidable part of learning.** To become more effective public and foreign policy has to involve a process of discovery that requires a greater readiness by citizens and practitioners to accept risk, and to learn from failure. This is crucial in any field of human endeavour.

3. **Self-awareness.** As citizens and leaders take on greater individual responsibility this requires that they become more 'sovereign' over their political behaviour and opinions. Self-awareness is vital for politicians and diplomats: awareness of how easily we are conditioned and manipulated. We also need to learn how to avoid a sense of entitlement, whether as oppressor or victim.

4. **Mutual needs satisfaction.** All conflict negotiations involve working towards achieving mutual needs satisfaction between all parties. Actors manage competition and conflict without the need for one group to control or seek supremacy over another. This "eye-level" approach requires a capacity to

take on multiple perspectives without losing one's own, and accept that the needs of all sides should be met to the degree possible.

5. **Politics is a balancing act.** Individual and collective needs require to be constantly balanced, within and between nations. This is a dynamic equation and recognizing of that reality involves a willingness to be flexible and preparedness to constantly adapt and readapt.

6. **Understanding human motivation.** The above principles require greater knowledge and better understanding of human motivations in order to be realized – we cannot just take a leap to get to them. High emotional states, cultural conditioning, and aspects of group behaviour that obstruct effective political solutions from being pursued need to be better understood and mastered. By assimilating such new knowledge, public policymaking can gradually be redefined, and its practice substantially improved, to the benefit of the body politic.

    We should always bring back policy making to the question of 'how well will any action we take sensibly meet the innate physical and emotional needs of everyone involved'.

7. **Wisdom in leadership.** Without common sense there can be no wisdom because under those conditions it cannot find expression. In these increasingly challenging times, dedication to excellence in the craft of wise politics and diplomacy is essential as is the application of common sense.

The Conciliators Guild's Commitment

Members of the Guild commit that it should remain an independent forum (uncorrupted by private or national agendas), and will reach out to other individuals and organizations that recognize and support its principles.

The Guild commits to assist members who agree to the above principles and their furtherance by

i) maintaining and expanding the network

ii) convening members physically, rather than virtually, to the degree that finances permit

iii) regularly disseminating knowledge through the website, courses, and discussions with members

iv) consulting with members about the ideas and their application.

Membership to the Guild is by invitation or recommendation. However, if you support its principles, you may apply to join and be considered for invitation or seek an existing member to recommend you.

The membership fee is kept low to encourage people entering relevant professions to join so they can learn from the best.